Health Facility Malpractice Cases:

A Management Prevention Guide

Health Facility Malpractice Cases:

A Management Prevention Guide

Monroe M. Title and William A. Rothman

Nova Science Publishers, Inc.
Commack

Art Director: Maria Ester Hawrys
Assistant Director: Elenor Kallberg
Graphics: Denise Dieterich, Kerri Pfister,
Erika Cassutti and Barbara Minerd
Manuscript Coordinator: Roseann Pena
Book Production: Tammy Sauter, Benjamin Fung
Circulation: Irene Kwartiroff and Annette Hellinger

Library of Congress Cataloging-in-Publication Data

Title, Monroe M.
Health facility malpractice cases: a management prevention guide/ Monroe M. Title, William A. Rothman.
p. cm.
Includes bibliographical references and index.
ISBN 1-56072-227-4 (library binding)
1. Medical personnel—Malpractice—United States. 2. Health facilities—Risk management—United States—Case studies.
I. Title, Monroe M. II. Title
KF2905.3.R68 1995 346.7303'32—dc20
[347.306332] 95-8061
CIP

6080 Jericho Turnpike, Suite 207
Commack, New York 11725
Tele. 516-499-3103 Fax 516-499-3146
E Mail Novascil@aol.com

Printed in the United States of America

CONTENTS

What This Book Will Do for You

The purpose of this book is to provide a comprehensive survey of the issues and developments in health care agencies which lead to malpractice lawsuits, using case studies and risk management analyses. By carefully analyzing standards of care, departures from the standards of care, and results of litigation the book aims to show how such problems can be avoided.

The book is unique in studying actual lawsuits and their results. It covers such suits as they affect hospitals, nursing homes and home health agencies.

Basically, the purpose of the book is to make the fundamentals of the law of hospital and institutional malpractice clear for quick understanding by anyone interested in the subject. We have attempted to reduce the technicalities to their basic simplicity.

Hospital and nursing home administrators are naturally very much concerned these days with the many malpractice claims and suits that are being made and brought against their institutions. We feel that there will be a steady growth in that trend until laws are passed to curb malpractice lawsuits. Administrators feel very strongly such claims in suits reflect seriously on the professional standing and abilities of the institutions they represent. Moreover, in a particular case, if a patient should win a large judgment, the effect could be disastrous upon the financial resources of the institution if they are not fully protected by insurance.

Administrators want to understand the ways in which malpractice work. Many of them have vague ideas about them, which lack practical value. Up until now, there have not been more than a few isolated books on how to avoid malpractice. Even the average attorney finds it very burdensome to locate the various laws, regulations and background cases because they are scattered in many different ways. There are very few books on the subject of hospital malpractice and they tend to be rather technical, so that you cannot get the fundamentals clearly and quickly. What we want to do is present the basic elements so that you do not have to spend too much time or effort in the process of understanding malpractice, and this book, we believe, does that.

Attorneys as well as administrators should find this book very useful. Many of them have complained that there is little material on malpractice. By using case studies and citations, we feel that we have furnished attorneys and administrators with the fundamentals of hospital malpractice.

Administrators should realize that they should not handle malpractice suits or claims themselves. They should obtain the services of attorneys experienced in such cases.

Specifically, the book will discuss patients' rights and responsibilities; the doctrine of respondent superior; the handling of consents, especially the difference between implied consent and informed consent; the basics of nursing care to avoid malpractice; the credentialling of medical staff members and the granting of privileges to avoid malpractice; and such special problems as patient escapes, the issue of confidentially, liability, the statute of limitations, and the need for a safe working environment.

A special chapter concerns itself with personnel relationships and malpractice, dwelling especially on strikes, licensure, credentialling of employees and the duty to provide competent staff.

Finally, there is a chapter on the special issues of nursing homes as we are finding an increased number of cases against nursing homes.

In short, this book will tell you in simple language, the things you should know about institutional malpractice and the steps you have to take to avoid them in the future.

CHAPTER I

INTRODUCTION

Malpractice is generally conceived as a physician, nurse or other caregiver providing services that result in a poor and unexpected outcome. Many health care administrators feel that, although the care their staff renders should be the best, when things go wrong it really doesn't affect them. This book's purpose is to change that feeling. When care goes wrong everyone, including the institution, is affected. The iatrogenic changes brought about by lack of maintaining community standards, by poor quality control, by ignoring staffing evaluation and through poor management can have serious consequences for the health care facility.

This book is intended to point out to the administrator examples of what kinds of problems they may encounter in their working environment. By reviewing the cases presented it is hoped that lessons can be learned for the administrative staff to establish total quality management procedures so that similar problems may be avoided within their own jurisdictions. This book differs in one major respect from other publications which we have examined. We have included many cases quoting the actual court records. We have done so in order to apprise the administrator of what a judge actually views as the most important attributes of a mismanaged situation. How a judge actually interprets, discusses and decides cases - what he or she sees as the relevant facts and salient factors of a case - is important to understand in order to establish a risk management program. By carefully reviewing the judges comments the executive can, hopefully, set up procedures and processes that will avoid similar difficulties and lapses in their institutions.

Some of the cases have also been presented in the form of how an expert witness will review and summarize a case when asked to review a proposed law suit by an attorney. The expert witness who is familiar with administrative medicine procedures is presented with the medical and hospital records and from that information, utilizing an understanding of the prevailing standards of care in a community reaches a conclusion for an attorney on the merits of the case. It is important for the health care manager to understand this process too as it points the way to providing high quality record keeping, which in turn leads to protecting the institution and its staff.

A third method utilized in this book is a simple narrative of a case to further illustrate some of the major problems one can expect to encounter. Although these additional narratives are not presented in an extensive format they are used to indicate different nuances in cases that have been discussed in detail.

In most of the cases, the "standard of care" is referred to. It is essential that the administrator understand the concept of standard of care. The question that is often asked of expert witnesses in hospital and nursing home malpractice cases is "What is the standard of care?" This has been defined in several cases. For example:

> "The proper standard of care expected of a hospital staff toward hospital patients is such reasonable care and attention for their safety as their mental and physical condition require."[1]

And in another case a comment was made in a case that:

> "The internal rules and regulations of a hospital do not establish the applicable standard of care which should be met by a hospital and the staff for purposes of determining liability in a malpractice sanction."[2]

---

[1] McClaine v. Alger, 150 Michigan App 306, 388NW 2nd 249.

[2] Gallagher v. Detroit Macomb Hospital Association, 171 Michigan App 761, 431 NW 2nd 90.

The above, however, is still vague and we feel should be elaborated. A standard is not necessarily that which represents the ideal. It may reflect only that which legally constituted, responsible, authoritative bodies deemed to be to the welfare of the public, and which is reasonably obtainable in the light of generally accepted ethics, competencies, methods and resources. The degree toward which the standard aspires to the ideal may be on an ascending scale, with the final result poor at one end of the scale and excellent at the other end of the spectrum, the later being the ultimate objective.

Considered in another way, a standard may be said to be a measure of quality established on a voluntary basis by those subject to it, or imposed upon them by a legal authority.

Most obvious of the standards are those which are mandatory, closely followed by the recommendations of the regulatory bodies which issue the mandatory standards. It is suspected that the usual "recommendation" of such a body is really intended to be construed only as a shade less emphatic than those that are listed as mandatory. Next to consider are the suggestions of regulatory and enforcement agencies. Such suggestions also may be presented as a result of the request for advice on the part of the operators of institutions. These operator requests usually reflect management aspiration toward self-education and appraisal and may follow a consultant's evaluation of institutional resources. Or they may come as a result of an out-of-schedule inspection by an official agency invited to review principles, standards, policies, methods and competencies by the institution wishing to exceed minimum standards.

Governmentally imposed standards based upon law are usually minimum, the starting point for the development of higher levels for an individual institution. The voluntary standard is supplementary to the mandatory standard and constitutes one of the most important indices of the institution's desire to serve its clientele to the best of its ability, in a safe and efficient manner, for government regulations, on any level, while they may point toward the ideal, generally proclaim only minimum standards.

On the other hand, the voluntary standard should not and generally does not seek a merely acceptable minimum. It serves to stimulate the operator to the highest level of service to which he or she is capable.

The basis for a body of excellent voluntary standards, as well as for enthusiastic compliance for those that are mandatory, is always the attitude of the governing body of an institution.

In addition, it is the wise administrator who seeks to convey to his/her staff and to the governing body the real need for maximum development of voluntary standards as well as compliance for those that are mandatory. In turn, the governing body, desiring excellent care, cannot but support its administrative representatives in their effort toward the attainment of this objective. Even more important, the governing body will wish to give maximum support to the administration which seeks through education, evaluation and continuous reappraisal the establishment of standards which approach the ideal.

The standards, both mandatory and voluntary, must be in harmony with the total objectives and mission of the institution. This is the burden of administration, but it must be assisted by all concerned.

However eager the institution may be for high standards, the rank and file employees, by and large, will go their separate ways unless concerted, indeed concentrated, effort is made to help them wish to observe high standards in the performance of their work and to maintain a continuously improving level of efficiency.

Hospitals must learn that they must be prepared to give humanitarian services as well as scientific service. Through improvement of the organization of hospitals and with proper utilization of existing facilities and personnel, much can be done to improve the quality of service rendered to patients.[3]

The hospital finds it an advantage administratively, socially, and economically to be a standardized institution. Standardization means a more complete and efficiently functioning organization as a whole. The standard for hospitals provides the hospital with fundamental principles pertaining to the best plan for assuring good professional care to patients. The carrying out of these principles

---

[3] McGibony, Principles of Hospital Administration, pp 96-99.

gives better assurance that the administration is functioning in a manner that best fulfills its purpose.[4] One final caveat is important and that is that the patient is an individual and different from other patients and cannot be standardized.

It is particularly important for hospitals to pay attention to mishaps and to have a program in place that can monitor the quality and quantity of care that has been rendered. A recent study shows that hospitals appear to have fewer and less severe malpractice claims if they "educated physicians and nurses about their role in risk management; had a policy of informing the clinical chief of staff when an adverse event occurred in his or her department (and) maintained a hospital board committee for overseeing risk management and provided the board with regular reports."[5] This study also found that in hospitals in Maryland that had a policy to communicate effectively with the chief clinicians the average amount of claim awarded was six times less than in those hospitals without such a policy.

Good communication with staff and employees is a key element in total quality management. Not only is that shown in the above study but, as can be seen by reviewing Chapter 9, it is a very important element in good employee relations. It is also true in the staff to staff relationships and in staff to patient relations.

In studying mistakes housestaff had made in caring for patients, 54% of interns and residents reported that they had made the errors because they felt they lacked information that they should have know. (51% said they had too many other tasks to perform and 41% reported that the mistakes were caused by fatigue.) 46% of the cases were never discussed with their supervisors and only 24% of cases were discussed with the patient or members of the patients families. Some of the medical residents felt that they were not discussed due to their belief that the hospitals administra-

---

[4] Ibid. page 100.

[5] "Objective measures prove value of risk management." Terese Hudson, Hospitals, 65:34+, September 20, 1991.

tors were too "judgemental" and that the "atmosphere" of the institution inhibited such discussion.[6]

It is generally felt (but not proven as far as these writers know) that most malpractice suits are brought about because of patient anger. The American Hospital Association has advised physicians that they can control some adverse problems that arise by "treating the patient with dignity, keeping the patient and family informed, being available when needed, communicating with other doctors and nurses in the patients' interest, not contributing to unreasonable expectations (and) documenting carefully."[7]

One of the problems that administrators face is the fear that employees and medical staff have in admitting that they have done something wrong. They do not want to report an adverse reaction, a medication error, a poor outcome or an improper procedure for fear of managerial retaliation. It is, therefore, up to the top executive staff who wish to operate within a total quality management program to establish an atmosphere of trust and cooperation so as to remove the fears of the staff. It is not within the scope of this book to delineate risk management guidelines. However, it is essential to point out that in a total quality management program managing the prevention of risk is a key element. All accidents and incidents must be reported and analyzed to learn what has happened, what caused it to happen and how to prevent its recurrence.

The hospital, as well as all health care facilities, have a legal role as well as other duties to perform. As Selby, et al have indicated:[8]

> "The hospital in its various roles of health care provider, employer and corporate entity has certain common law duties to the patient. These duties include the following;

[6] Wu, A.W.; Folkman, S.; McPhee, S.J. and Lo, B. "Do house officers learn from their mistakes." JAMA 265:2089-94, April 24, 1991.

[7] Risk management pearls for physicians. Chicago, American Society for Healthcare Risk Management of the American Hospital Association, 1991. page 2.

[8] Selby, Myra C. et al. Hospital and Physician Liability: A Legal and Risk Management Overview. Washington, National Health Lawyers Association, 1992. pages 82-83.

A. The duty to have competent, qualified physicians on the medical staff;
B. The duty to have competent and appropriately trained non-physician personnel;
C. The duty to have and follow appropriate policies and procedures;
D. The duty to provide appropriate equipment, supplies and machines;"

What factors contribute to negligence? In a study by Harvard researchers it was found that negligent events "differ markedly from hospital to hospital. Ten-fold differences among individual hospitals were found when patient's age and diagnosis were taken into account. The number of adverse events due to negligence was five percent higher in government hospitals than in non-profit hospitals and three times greater than in proprietary hospitals."[9] The study also found that in University teaching hospitals the events caused by negligent medical care are only half of those found in the non-teaching facilities. This difference in lower negligence rates was "attributed to more and better supervision within these hospitals because of their teaching mission and their state-of-the-art medical technology."[10] Hospitals with a predominent number of minority patients and hospitals that are under-capitalized also were found to have "significantly higher negligence rates."[11]

Further study results also indicate that "adverse events are split almost evenly between operative and non-operative procedures; however, the percentage of adverse events caused by negligence is lower among surgical patients than non-surgical patients (17 vs. 37 percent). Among non-operative adverse events, drug-related problems are the leading cause of medical injury. Antibiotics, oncologic drugs and anticoagulants are the three categories of drugs responsible for the majority of drug-related adverse events...(T)he study findings also revealed the hospital emergency room as a real 'hot-

---

[9] "Negligent medical care: what is it, where is it, and how widespread is it?" ABridge: A Special edition from the Robert Wood Johnson Foundation. Spring, 1991, page 6.

[10] Ibid, page 7.

[11] Ibid.

spot' for negligence... 70 percent of adverse events in the emergency room were due to negligence. Hospital emergency rooms heavily used by patients as primary care clinics are a major source of adverse events because of poor follow-up.[12]

Additional research disclosed that "patient management errors were cited most frequently as associated with claims of negligence. Technical performance problems like surgical 'slips' accounted for one-third to one-half of injuries in all specialties except radiology. Only 6% to 11% of negligence claims were the result of medical and nursing staff coordination problems. Less than 15% of negligence claims were associated with failure to order diagnostic tests or employ monitoring techniques.

> "Obstetrical negligence claims most often stemmed from errors in physician judgment, whereas gynecologic claims were more likely the result of inadequate technical performance. General surgery claims were roughly evenly divided between patient management and technical performance errors. In anesthesiology, the majority of negligence claims stemmed from performance errors rather than improper monitoring. Diagnostic errors accounted for the vast majority of radiology claims."[13]

A specific study concerning hospital risk factors has also been reported. This study showed[14] that as the average daily census in a hospital rises, the number of claims rises; yearly claims costs increased by $644 for each additional patient in the census; for each additional patient in the average daily census of an intensive care unit, annual claims costs increased $2, 651-four times the malpractice expenses of standard care." Childrens' hospitals and for-profit hospitals claims costs were much greater than the average, as was the presence of a level 3 Neonatal intensive Care Unit.

All of these studies point out the necessity of a total quality management program which includes an aggressive risk manage-

---

[12] Ibid.

[13] ABridge; Advances. Newsletter of the Robert Wood Johnson Foundation. Spring, 1992, page 6.

[14] Ibid, page 8.

ment program. Such a program includes identification of the individuals who are constantly making errors as well as a continuous review of the processes and procedures of the institution. To assist in the first step Congress has established the National Practitioner Data Bank which was mandated as part of the Health Care Quality Improvement Act of 1986 and became operational as of September 1, 1990. The purpose of the bank is "to keep tabs on possible malpractice and professional misbehavior by physicians... and prevent them from concealing a damaging history by moving from state to state."[15]

Under the Act, hospitals are required to report any actions taken to restrict or remove a physicians clinical privileges for any period exceeding 30 days. Any malpractice settlements and any licensure actions taken by a state licensing board which may relate to a physician's professional competence or conduct must also be reported. The Bank is to set up physician profiles (and thus ultimately the community standard of care) and hospitals are required to check with the Data bank as a specific part of the initial credentialling process and at least once every two years. Failure for the hospital to do so could result in a $10,000 fine. If a malpractice action arises and the hospital has not checked with the Bank the hospital will be held liable as if it had known all of the Bank's information when appointment of the physician was made.

It is hoped that by reviewing the cases presented in this book, administrators will be able to have a guidepost in establishing an important piece of a total quality management program with their facilities and allow for a workable and successful risk management service.

---

[15] Gordon, E. "Questions abound as start-up nears for physician data bank." Modern Healthcare, July 2, 1990, pages 28-30.

CHAPTER II

RESPONDEAT SUPERIOR

Respondeat Superior is a legal principle which holds that the employer is legally responsible for its employees. (In legalese language it is that the "master" is held answerable for the acts of his "servants.")

From a liability standpoint it must be determined if the person treating a patient is the agent (and therefore the "servant") of the institution. Such a determination is made by discovering if the health care facility exercises some actual control over the acts of the clinician. If the clinician is an employee of the facility then control is generally assumed to exist. The employer is held responsible for its employee as long as the employee's act was done in the course of employment. Authority over the employee is either expressed or implied.

The employer can be held liable even if it has done nothing wrong itself. If, for example, a pharmacist who is employed by a hospital dispenses the wrong medication to a patient and the patient suffers from the error, the hospital may be held liable even if the pharmacist was properly trained, selected with great care and was working within his area of responsibility. If, however, an employee does an improper thing during the course of his employment which was not done under his employees authority, the employer is not liable. (In this book we are using the term "employer" as synonymous with "institution" and/or "facility".)

The cases which follow illustrate typical respondeat superior situations. In order to get an idea of how a judge approaches the issue of respondeat superior let us start with the case of Jessica Shumaker vs (among others) the Caswell Family Medical Center, Inc. Caswell Family Medical Center (CFMC) is a rural family practice clinic in North Carolina. Physicians practicing there are assigned by the National Health Service Corporation in order to fulfill an obligation to the United States Government which paid for the physicians medical education. The case was heard in the United States District Court in Greensboro, North Carolina in July, 1988. Pertinent excerpts from the official record follow:

> "The action arises from alleged medical malpractice by two doctors, Gahear F. Hamlor and David W. Johnson, in failing to refer Jessica Shumaker to an ophthalmologist. Plaintiffs Jessica and her parents allege that as a result of the doctors' alleged negligence, and the allegedly negligent failure of Caswell Family Medical Center to supervise the doctors and to implement a quality assurance program, diagnosis and treatment of Jessica's bilateral retinoblastomas (cancerous tumors in the eyes) was delayed, reducing her chances of retaining her vision and ultimately necessitating the enucleation of both of her eyes.
>
> "...Dr. Johnson... practiced at Caswell Family Medical Center ("CFMC") to fulfill his NHSC obligation but did so on a private contract basis and Plaintiffs did not allege liability of the United States for Dr. Johnson's actions. CFMC is named as a defendant for the negligence of Drs. Johnson and Hamlor under the theory of respondeat superior. In addition, Plaintiffs also made claims against CFMC for its independent negligence in failing to supervise the doctors, institute a quality assurance program, or maintain proper patient records.
>
> "...Facts
>
> "Jessica Shumaker was born in Caswell County, North Carolina, on February 17, 1981. Beginning in March 1981 and continuing periodically through at least November 1982 Jessica's parents brought her to the Caswell Family Medical Center in Yanceyville, Caswell County, North Carolina, for well-baby and minor illness related examinations. Caswell County is a designated health manpower shortage area under 42 C.F.R. par 23, and CFMC is a

rural family practice clinic intended to supply basic health care to citizens of the county. CFMC, a federal-grant-funded center, was periodically assigned doctors through the NHSC. Dr. Hamlor fulfilled a two-year commitment to NHSC by practicing from 1980 until August 1982. During that time his paychecks, vacation time, and continuing medical education were handled through NHSC. Between March 1981 and July 26, 1982, Dr. Hamlor, who was a certified family practitioner, examined Jessica at CFMC on numerous occasions.

"Jessica's mother... claims that starting in August 19, she noticed that Jessica's left eye would wander, rather than focusing in conjunction with the right eye. Mrs. Shumaker alleges that she brought this condition to Dr. Hamlor's attention on numerous occasions, during regular visits to CFMC, and Dr. Hamlor passed the problem off as a "lazy eye" and said if it did not correct itself by the time Jessica turned two years old they would correct it by patching her right eye. Neither CFMC's records nor any other notes by Dr. Hamlor indicated complaints about Jessica's eyes or that Dr. Hamlor examined her eyes. Plaintiffs nevertheless assert that the problem worsened over time but Dr. Hamlor's advice remained the same.

"Dr. Johnson is a general practitioner who came to CFMC September 1982 to fulfill a commitment to NHSC under the "private practice option." Upon placement at CFMC Dr. Johnson entered into an "Agreement to Provide Professional Services" with CFMC through its project director... From September through November or December 1982, Dr. Johnson saw Jessica several times. (Jessica's mother) asserts that she called Jessica's wandering eye to Dr. Johnson's attention and also informed him of Dr. Hamlor's diagnosis that it was simply "lazy eye." Dr. Johnson concurred in this diagnosis and did not refer Plaintiffs to an ophthalmologist. Dr. Johnson contends that he reviewed Dr. Hamlor's notes on his patients which do not indicate anything about Jessica's eyes.

"In late December 1982 or early January 1983, (Jessica's mother) visited her optometrist, Dr. B. Daniel Jason, for herself, and while there requested that he see Jessica. Dr. Jason looked at Jessica in his waiting room, without the use of any instruments and "sensed" that she had a more serious problem with her eyes. He referred her to Dr. Charles C. Freed, an ophthalmologist in Danville, Virginia, which is approximately 15 miles from

Yanceyville. Dr. Freed examined Jessica on January 14, 1983, under anesthesia, and made the initial diagnosis of retinoblastoma. He then referred her to Dr. Thomas C. Kerns, Jr., at McPherson Hospital in Durham, North Carolina. Dr. Kerns examined Jessica on January 19, 1983, concurred in the diagnosis, and referred her immediately for treatment to Dr. Robert M. Ellsworth at the Cornell University Medical School, Sloan-Kettering Hospital in New York City. Dr. Ellsworth is recognized by experts for both sides as one of the foremost experts, if not the foremost expert, on treatment of retinoblastoma.

"Dr. Ellsworth observed several cancerous lesions in each of Jessica's eyes and began radiation treatments and then cryotherapy (freezing). Dr. Ellsworth apparently believed that there remained a good chance of saving the eyes, either a two in three chance, or perhaps a 35% chance of saving the left eye and a 60%-70% chance of saving the right eye. From Dr. Ellsworth's comments the treatment seemed to be proceeding well for a time, but gradually Jessica lost sight in her left eye, which was removed on November 11, 1983. Subsequent treatment of the right eye also failed, and on February 23, 1984, it was removed.

"Jessica's cancer apparently did not metastasize prior to enucleation and she is currently healthy, but without sight.

"Discussion

"...In order to recover on a medical malpractice claim, the Plaintiff must prove three elements founded in general principles of negligence: (1) the applicable standard of care; (2) Defendant's breach of that standard; and (3) the casual relationship between Defendant's breach and the Plaintiff's injury.

"...In this case the voluminous deposition testimony submitted sufficiently explores the standards of care applicable to Drs. Hamlor and Johnson, and raises a genuine issue regarding their compliance with these standards.

"...The record before the court does not include any evidence that either Dr. Hamlor or Dr. Johnson ever referred the Plaintiffs to an opthalmologist (sic), nor is there any significant mention of Jessica's eye problem in Jessica's records, prior to January 1983. Therefore, the disputed factual issue of whether the Plaintiffs repeatedly complained to the doctors about Jessica's wandering or "lazy" eye is material to the question of whether Dr. Hamlor and Dr. Johnson satisfied the standard of care.

"...Standard of care for CFMC

"CFMC contends that the materials before the court do not establish a standard of care applicable to a small, rural health clinic; therefore summary judgment should be granted to CFMC on the claims alleging its independent negligence. The Plaintiffs assert that CFMC was negligent in failing to supervise the doctors and in not establishing a quality assurance program which would have implemented formal record keeping and review procedures.

"...(A)ssuming that CFMC is a health care provider its conduct may be scrutinized under a standard of due care, in addition to the statutory standard.

"...(T)he materials in the record suggest a genuine issue regarding CFMC's negligence. The court especially notes the statements of Dr. Thomas A. Cable, a member of the in-house committee for the Family Practice Center at Moses H. Cone Hospital, regarding compliance with any applicable federal guidelines and with a quality assurance program. Dr. Cable emphasized the importance of review procedures, particularly over young physicians. ...Although Dr. Cable stated that not all small practices have formal or informal review of physicians, ...and that a two-person practice clinic need not have organized chart reviews, ...he also said that if there are federal guidelines to be met or exceeded... Dr. Cable maintained that where an entity has a quality assurance program, designed to ensure proper patient care, its procedures should be followed... Finally, Dr. Cable stressed the need in medical facilities with substantial turnover of medical personnel to have good, standard charting procedures and for doctors to verbally apprise successor physicians of any chronic cases.

"...Under the Principles of Practice which CFMC developed, the staff was to review on-site services, examine samples of patient records, and follow the quality assurance plan. However, whether the existing plan was actually implemented and followed remains a disputed question of fact.

"...Expert testimony is usually required to show that the defendant's negligence was more likely than not the cause of the injury... The parties essentially agree that with respect to the negligence of Drs. Hamlor and Johnson the existence of a genuine issue regarding causation depends on the testimony of Dr. Robert Ellsworth.

"...Taking the evidence in the light most favorable to the Plaintiffs and allowing them all reasonable inferences therefrom, the court finds that Dr. Ellsworth's testimony raises a genuine issue regarding the casual link between the alleged negligence of Dr. Hamlor and Johnson and Plaintiff's injuries.

"...With respect to the independent negligence claims against CFMC, an issue exists as to whether proper review procedures and a quality assurance plan would have allayed the effects of the doctor's conduct.

"...Respondeat Superior

"CFMC seeks summary judgment on Plaintiffs' claims which attempt to hold CFMC liable for the doctors' negligence. CFMC asserts that Dr. Hamlor was employed by the NHSC and was not CFMC's "agent." CFMC also contends that Dr. Johnson, who chose the private practice option offered by the NHSC, was an independent contractor whose actions cannot be attributed to the clinic.

"The rule of respondeat superior holds an employer, including a medical facility, liable for the acts of its agents committed in the course and scope of their employment.

"...Any negligence by Dr. Hamlor or Dr. Johnson obviously occurred during the course of Jessica's care at CFMC. Therefore, the question is whether the doctors were CFMC's agents. For the purpose of imposing vicarious liability, whether the requisite agency relationship existed depends on the degree of control CFMC exercised over the doctors' activities.

"...The nature of the relationship between CFMC and Dr. Johnson remains in dispute. The written "Agreement to Provide Professional Services" (Agreement") which the two entered into calls Dr. Johnson an independent contractor, ...but this is not conclusive under North Carolina law... The contract also provided that Dr. Johnson would work normal hours and exercise independent judgment.

"...On the other hand(it)... also restricts Dr. Johnson to working for CFMC. In addition, CFMC was to pay his compensation... including vacation and continuing medical education,... his disability,... and even some of his moving expenses... Finally, the contract included a non-competition clause.

"...(T)he state court of appeals found the requisite agency relationship when the doctor's contract required him to work set hours, made provisions for vacation and sick leave, and limited him to practicing at that hospital. (Note: this refers to a previous case.)

"...Even disregarding for the moment the disagreement between CFMC administrator Stephen Shore and Dr. Johnson about whether Dr. Johnson's contract required him to make public appearances and to entertain on behalf of CFMC, the remaining provisions of his professional contract certainly raise some question under North Carolina law about whether he was an independent contractor or an employee. Therefore, summary judgment for CFMC as to the claims against Dr. Johnson (for which summary judgment has been discussed above) is also denied.

"...In contrast, the record supports CFMC's position that Dr. Hamlor was an employee of NHSC, and was not CFMC's agent. Applying the "extent of control" standard, Dr. Hamlor's situation is substantially different because he did not elect the private practice option in fulfilling his commitment to NHSC.

"...Moreover, CFMC did not exercise any significant degree of control over Dr. Hamlor other than the general guidelines and procedures to be followed at the clinic which were outlined in the Principles of Practice between Dr. Hamlor and CFMC.

"...In short, the only control CFMC exerted over Dr. Hamlor was administrative, e.g., the day-to-day scheduling and billing of patients, and CFMC was required to reimburse NHSC for Dr. Hamlor's time. CFMC's responsibility as a health center was to supervise its medical personnel and operations in terms of care and administration. It did not directly control the government physicians beyond the general terms of the Principles of Practice. Because of its lack of legal control over Dr. Hamlor, CFMC should not be held vicariously responsible for his negligence and its motion for summary judgment on this claim is granted.

"...SUMMARY

"In response to Defendant CFMC's request in its brief that the court clarify the remaining issues for trial, the court will summarize today's ruling. The court finds sufficient evidence in the record to raise genuine issues about Dr. Hamlor's and Dr. Johnson's breach of the standard of care, and the connection between such alleged breaches and the injuries suffered by Plaintiffs. That harm may include both the ultimate loss of Jessica's eyesight and the lost possibility of recovery she may have suffered due to the allegedly negligent delay in diagnosis and treatment. The court also finds that the "Agreement to Provide Professional Services" and testimony regarding Dr. Johnson's role at CFMC raise the issue of Dr. Johnson's status as an agent of CFMC, and CFMC's vicarious liability for his negligence. Finally, the court finds just enough evidence of the standard or standards of care applicable to CFMC, breach of those standards, and causation from such breach to make summary judgment on Plaintiffs' claim of independent negligence by CFMC inappropriate.

"The court finds that the documentary and deposition evidence concerning Dr. Hamlor's relationship with CFMC would not allow a jury reasonably to find that CFMC exerted control sufficient to render Dr. Hamlor its agent. Accordingly, summary judgment is granted to CFMC on the claims asserting CFMC's vicarious liability for Dr. Hamlor's negligence. The court also finds no basis for Plaintiffs' claims that CFMC was negligent in hiring and holding out Dr. Johnson as qualified and summary judgment is granted on that claim as well.

"...ORDER AND JUDGMENT

"For the reasons set forth in the memorandum opinion filed contemporaneously herewith,

"IT IS ORDERED AND ADJUDGED that motion of Defendant and Third-Party Defendant Caswell Family Medical Center, Inc., for summary judgment is GRANTED in part and DENIED in part as follows: As to Plaintiff's claims seeking relief against Caswell Family Medical Center, Inc., on the basis of vicarious liability for the alleged negligence of Dr. Gahear Hamlor and as to Plaintiffs' claims seeking relief for Caswell Family Medical Center, Inc's independent negligence in hiring and holding out Defendant Dr. David Johnson as qualified, Defendant's motion for summary judgment is GRANTED and such claims of Plaintiffs against Caswell Family Medical Center, Inc, Defendant's motion for summary judgment is DENIED.

"IT IS FURTHER ORDERED that the motion of Defendant Dr. David Johnson for summary judgment is DENIED.

"IT IS FURTHER ORDERED that the motion of Defendant the United States of America for summary judgment is DENIED; and

"IT IS FURTHER ORDERED that the motion of Defendant the United States of America for judgment on the pleadings is DENIED."

As stated earlier, under the legal doctrine of Respondeat Superior, the employer is responsible for the actions of his employee. Thus, individual actions taken by nurses, laboratory personnel, respiratory therapists, etc. as well as interns and residents are considered the responsibility of the employer as long as they are working under their assigned duties. To illustrate this further, let us look at the following cases which were filed but settled before they got to court:

Mr. G was an 85 year old married male who was admitted to a Newark, New Jersey hospital on March 15, 1987 due to gastrointestinal bleeding. His principle diagnosis was carcinoma of the colon and it was noted in the record that he also had anemia and congestive heart failure. In 1976 he had a heart attack from which he had recovered. He also had several surgical procedures between 1976 and his 1987 admission into the hospital.

As a patient in the hospital he had an attending physician assisted by three other doctors, including an oncologist.

After performing many laboratory and xray tests and examinations it was the opinion of the physicians that surgery should be performed. Prior to and in preparation for surgery it was decided that Mr. G should receive two transfusions of packed red blood cells. He was given these transfusions in the morning of March 25, 1987 and again in the afternoon. 15 minutes after the administration of the second transfusion Mr. G died.

An autopsy performed on March 26th indicated that the cause of death was cardio-respiratory arrest following transfusion of incompatible blood. The manner of death was listed as accidental. The hospital record shows transfusion reaction as a secondary diagnosis.

Standards of Care

At the time of this incident good and accepted hospital practice required that hospital authorities do the following:

1. Maintain adequate controls on all laboratory tests including transfusion of blood and packed cells.

2. Patients should always be given the same type of blood as they currently have and precautions must be taken to ensure that the blood is compatible.

3. Arrangements must be made to properly identify hospital patients prior to any procedure. If two patients have the same name precautions must be taken to assure that they receive the correct meals, tests, xrays, medications, blood and packed blood cells. It is the duty of all hospital personnel including those in the laboratory and bloodbank to alert all staff having anything to do with administering tests that there are two or more patients with the same name as patients in the hospital. This can be done by the words "Name Alert" being hung on the bloodbank refrigerator door, for example, or an actual note indicating that precautions must be taken due to the fact that there are patients with similar names. A note might also be placed on the door of the room in which the patient resides indicating that there is another patient with a similar name in the hospital and cautioning staff to act accordingly.

4. An additional control should be instituted to prevent transfusion errors. Specifically, every patient has a medical record number and the number should be checked by the technician administering the blood by comparing the medical record number on the packed cells with the number on the patients medical record and with the number on the patients identification wrist band. (In discussing this case with bloodbank and surgical staff at other hospitals we learned that clerical error is the major cause of blood transfusion reactions.)

This hospital had a procedure which was very unusual: when a patient was transferred from one hospital unit to another the identification band on the patient's wrist was changed. Mr. G had been transferred from the third floor to a room in the comprehensive care unit on March 19th. When that occurred the admitting clerk pulled the record of one of the patients and made a new wrist band without realizing that there was also another patient with the same name in another part of the hospital. Thus the wrong medical record number was placed on the wristband of the patient who ultimately was to receive the transfusion of packed blood cells. When the staff administered the transfusion they probably thought they had the right patient because the numbers matched.

DEPARTURES FROM THE STANDARDS OF CARE

The personnel at the hospital departed from good and accepted hospital practice in the following ways:

From all indications they seem to have failed to institute a foolproof system of alerting personnel to the fact that patients with similar names were residing in the hospital. We do not know from the medical record if there was any type of "Name Alert" program. (And this would not normally be in a patients chart.) However, had there been a control, such as checking the name and the record number on the patients chart with the name and number on the packed cells, the chances of a mistake would have been minimized. We do not know if there was any system of alerting staff to the similarity of names on the bloodbank refrigerator. If such a "Name Alert" system existed the accident might have been averted. From the medical record we can ascertain that Mr. C had O positive blood. Patients with O positive must receive only O positive blood or packed cells. It is noted in the medical record that the patient received the first transfusion at 7:30 a.m., that his color was grayish, and that he had tremors over his entire body. He was alert and responsive but his entire bed was saturated with urine. This is a common occurrence when a blood reaction occurs. The death of the patient only 15 minutes after the second transfusion was completed is also a typical response to a transfusion error.

Under the doctrine of Respondeat Superior, the employer is responsible for the actions of his employees. In this instance, the hospital must be considered responsible for the actions of the nurses and laboratory personnel who administered the packed cells to Mr. G.

Causation

The failure to conform to good and accepted hospital practice was the probable cause of the injury to and the death of Mr. G. While he was an older man of 85 years, and was ready to undergo surgery which might have had several major risks involved, undoubtedly the error in administration of the packed cells hastened his death.

Conclusion

In the Spring of 1991, shortly before this case was to go to trial, the defendant, the hospital, admitted liability.

Case of Mrs. O

We next come to the case of a 34 year old black female admitted to the emergency room of a major hospital in the Detroit, Michigan area on September 11, 1987 with complaints of lower abdominal pain and vaginal spotting. She had been seen a week earlier at the office of a gynecologist who had diagnosed vaginal bleeding and nausea. On September 11th, this physician decided to perform a D and C in the emergency room of the hospital with the patient on a regular bed, not a surgical or gynecological bed. The hospital bed did not have side rails to secure the plaintiff. At some point during the procedure, Mrs. O, under the influence of anesthesia, fell off the bed onto the floor, striking her head as well as other parts of her body.

She had to be admitted to the hospital immediately thereafter and was examined for probable ectopic pregnancy. It was learned that she did indeed have a tubal pregnancy and received surgery. She remained in the hospital after her surgery, until September 15, 1987. She was subsequently seen by a neurologist with complaints of headaches, dizziness, memory difficulties and nervousness. The difficulties were traced to her fall. Other symptoms included blurred vision, nausea, lightheadiness, nosebleeds and tension. It should be noted that she previously was employed as a payroll clerk in one of the City of Detroit departments and was rated as an adequate employee. However, after her fall she had difficulties handling a full time position and she experienced post-traumatic incidents which lasted for 18 months.

STANDARDS OF CARE

In September 1987, good and accepted hospital practice require that the hospital authorities in this hospital do the following:

1. Establish adequate policies and procedures for emergency surgical patients to ensure proper treatment to avoid injury.
2. Properly evaluate and train its staff nurses, anesthetists and any other employees in the proper procedures for surgery performed under anesthesia. This patient was under anesthesia at the time of her fall.
3. Properly supervise employees and/or agents to ensure that the proper equipment is used.
4. Provide for the proper scrutiny, care and treatment of patients allowing them not to roll off of the beds while still under the influence of anesthesia.
5. Properly evaluate the qualifications of physicians not allowing any physician to perform surgery in a non-surgical setting.

DEPARTURES FROM THE STANDARD OF CARE

The hospital personnel and physicians at this hospital departed from good and accepted hospital practice in the following ways:

The hospital provided emergency service but failed to have a staff adequately watch patients in the emergency area. It did not establish adequate policies and procedures to provide proper treatment to patients and assure that they would not be injured in any way during the time they are in the emergency room. The hospital also failed to properly evaluate and train its staff nurses and other employees and agents in the way surgery should be performed under anesthesia and the way patients are taken care of in a surgical setting. This patient was not watched and was allowed to roll off the bed while still under the influence of anesthesia.

It should be noted that the patient was left on the bed while the nurse went out to get a stretcher, and it is believed that the doctor walked out of the room to finish his medical record which was located directly outside of the door to the room. It is at that time that the patient fell out of the bed. Certainly, the nurse could have called for help by simply pressing a call button located in the room and then asking another employee to come into the room and watch the patient or, alternatively, to get a stretcher so the patient could be transferred to a safer piece of equipment. The nurse also could have requested a nurse to stay with the patient while she was out getting the stretcher. In any event the patient did fall off the bed.

Furthermore, there were no side rails on the bed. Obviously a surgical bed should have been provided for a patient who was to have surgery in the emergency room. The patient had been put on an I.V. anesthesia and when she fell off the bed she suffered facial and head trauma.

Even if a regular stretcher or simple hospital bed was used someone should have been watching Mrs. O after she had her D&C so that she could not possibly fall off the bed and injure herself.

Under the doctrine of Respondeat Superior the employer is responsible for the actions of his employees. In this instance, the hospital must be considered responsible for the actions of its personnel in the emergency room as well as its physician agent.

CAUSATIONS

The failure to conform to good and accepted hospital practice was the probable cause of the injury to Mrs. O. From all indications she suffered severe head injuries, and may have suffered some brain damage. From the observations of psychologists who examined her almost a year subsequent to the fall, she apparently was still suffering the effects of her fall.

CONCLUSION

The case was settled out of court and was very favorable to the Plaintiff.

Case of Cardiac Arrest

The next case is that of a patient admitted to a hospital in the western section of Michigan in 1986. The patient was very ill and had been in and out of hospitals and nursing homes over a period of several years. He was in the intensive care unit in the Defendant hospital in February, 1986 when the incident occurred. Specifically, it was in the middle of the night as the patient was having difficulty breathing. He had a tube inserted in his trachea and apparently the tube was against the side of the trachea. The nurse, upon observing that the patient was having difficulty breathing, called for a resident and an intern. Despite the efforts of these housestaff physicians the patient went into cardiac arrest. By the time an attending physician appeared the patient was in very serious distress, and died shortly afterwards in another hospital to which he had been transferred. The following events had taken place:

1. The nurses failed to call the attending doctor or an internist on a timely basis. The last call for help was at 11:30 p.m. before the patient had cardiac distress. The patient continued to lose ground. All the notations in the medical record by the nursing and house staff indicate major changes occurred at 2 a.m., but it was difficult to handbag the patient. The staff were unable to insert a suction catheter to assist the patient (this occurred at 2:10 a.m.). At 3:45 a.m. the patient had more difficulty breathing and at 4 a.m. there was a further difficulty noted. However, the staff failed to communicate any of these changes to the attending physician or the internist. At 4:45 a.m. the patient went into cardiac arrest. The attending

physician had only been notified thirteen minutes prior to the arrest.

2. The nursing staff disregarded the rapid, shallow respirations and constant alerting by alarms which kept sounding. The ventilator connectors kept breaking off. At one time the patient was so agitated he grabbed a nurse's throat. Yet the nurses gave increased doses of valium and morphine without asking a physician. The attending physician and the internist indicated that they would have come into the hospital had they been notified.

3. There were abnormal blood gas tests after midnight but these were only reported to the house staff and not the attending physician. The attending doctors felt they should have been told of the test results.

4. There were very serious abnormal study results reported by another hospital which had previously taken care of the patient. The results of these studies were not relayed to the attending physician when they were received by the hospital.

Standards of Care

The standards of care would have called for the attending physician and internist to be informed of the patient's difficulties, especially when the patient's condition kept deteriorating and he was rapidly losing ground. It is the responsibility of a nurse and a house physician to notify an attending doctor or a specialist when a patient keeps losing ground and his condition keeps deteriorating. Failure to do so undoubtedly led to the cardiac arrest and the patient's subsequent death.

Conclusion

This case will be settled favorably to the widow of the patient. The Defendant hospital is liable for its employees under the legal theory of Respondeat Superior.

Case of Mr. B

Mr. B was an elderly man who was up and about in a long term care unit of a Veterans Hospital in the eastern part of Michigan. One evening, he attended a bingo game in the hospital at about 6:30 p.m. and then failed to return to his room by 9:30 p.m. Security was called and they searched for him but could not locate him. Early the next morning his son called and he, in turn, notified the police that his father was missing. The body of Mr. B was found the next morning, not too far from the hospital, frozen to death. It was felt that the long term facility was negligent in not moving faster to locate the patient, and certainly, in not preventing him from leaving the unit.

Standards of Care

Elopement refers to patients leaving a facility without supervision or knowledge of the staff. To prevent elopement of patients, long term care facilities have to consider the adoption of the following:

1. Review and revise all of the patient care plans to reflect each patients current needs. Emphasis should be given to problems for patients having histories of confusion or potential for elopement.
2. Educate all facility staff of their roles in providing care to these patients and the monitoring of these patients to their safety. Perhaps the family can be notified to help out in this regard.
3. On each shift, be sure the nurses' aides and appropriate staff are being utilized effectively to provide care and the monitoring for each patient's needs.
4. Make sure all of the staff are aware of their specific duties and responsibilities: the need for the staff to be alert when exit door buzzers sound; and accountability for care supervision provided to the patient.
5. A policy and procedure should be developed specific to elopement. This should include a procedure for the appropriate

method for conducting a search inside and outside the facility in the event that a patient is reported as missing. All employees should receive in service education and updated on a regular basis on this policy and procedure to ensure that all staff are kept current.

Conclusion

This case involved negligence in carrying out an elopement policy. Under the theory of Respondeat Superior, the hospital was liable for the actions of its employees. This case was settled for $200,000, the maximum allowed by Federal Law.

Discussion

The five cases presented here show that it is exceptionally important for health care administrators to select their personnel judicially, and once they have been selected, to supervise them with equal care. It is evident that the doctrine of Respondeat Superior puts the health care facility at total risk for the misdeeds of its staff. In each of these cases the hospital was responsible in one way or another for the actions of its employees. It is, of course, impossible from a managerial standpoint to oversee the actions of every individual working while that work is being accomplished.

After an initial period of work in which the new worker can be evaluated it is assumed that the employee will carry out his duties properly and within the boundaries set by the facility for doing the work. A problem exists in delivering health care, however, in as much as the delivery of that care is both an art and a science. Thus, because it is an art it requires individual judgment on the part of the clinician delivering the care. Such judgment cannot be defined before hand as judgment must develop as circumstances arise. Such factors as the patients age, social standing, sociological background, family, religion, politics, etc. as well as the nature and complexities of his illness all will determine how the clinician feels the patients problems should be handled. Because of the innumerable configurations of these factors it is not possible to have a definitive methodology of how to proceed in each and every case. Thus, the art of care plays a large role in how to treat. We have seen in the above cases that the one prevailing determination which the courts use in deciding malpractice is that of the "community standard." (That is, given the circumstances of the case was the standard of the community followed?)

Even though the administrators of a facility cannot oversee every procedure that is being done they can, and must, see that the community standards are met. This can best be accomplished through the process of Total Quality Management (TQM). It is the duty of the administration to involve all staff including the physicians (even if the physicians are not employees) in providing quality service.

Total Quality Management is a concept that encompasses the belief that quality will be obtained by incorporating quality planning, quality control and then quality improvement.[1] It is up to the administration to create the atmosphere for quality and once created to participate actively in establishing an institutional culture that will involve all personnel in the quest for quality.

It is acknowledged that unfortunate lapses in quality care will occur due to accidents, serendipity, etc. but when such problems do arise they should be discussed fully and freely with everyone in the institution so that steps may be taken to erect barriers to avoid similar problems from recurring.

The concept of TQM involves having all staff, and particularly higher management available to review, discuss and derive conclusions about all aspects of care. All staff should agree on the methodology to be taken to solve a particular problem. Once such agreement is reached staff must be informed and the procedures established and followed. It is up to management to make sure that all staff are aware of those procedures. New personnel must be educated concerning the institution's methods through orientation

---

[1] Sahney, Vinod K. and Warden, Gail L. "The Quest for Quality and Productivity in Health Services." Frontiers of Health Services Management. 7:2-40, Summer, 1991.

sessions. Such procedures should also be reviewed at least yearly and it should be mandatory for all staff to attend such annual review sessions.

Total Quality cannot be obtained through management by complacency. Administration must be deeply involved in and committed to the process for it to succeed.

In order to protect the hospital and nursing home from liability a number of precautions seem essential:

1. Carefully check the background of all potential employees. This means not only utilizing proper interviewing techniques, but diligent checking of applicants past work records.

2. Make absolutely sure that the applicant, if required to be licensed, has a current license. Once an individual is hired it is essential that a system be established to check on renewal of licensure (generally a yearly requirement of the state.)

3. Upon hiring a physician and at each subsequent reappointment date, it is necessary under the terms of the National Healthcare Quality Improvement Act of 1986 to check with the National Practitioner Data Bank. The Data Bank has been established by Congressional action to keep tabs on possible malpractice and professional misbehavior by physicians and to prevent them from concealing a damaging history by having them move from state to state. It should be noted that hospitals are *required* to check with the Data Bank as part of the regular credentialling process. Failure for the hospital to check could result in a fine of as much as $10,000. If a malpractice action does occur and the hospital has been found not to have checked with the Data Bank the hospital will be liable as if it had checked and had known the information in the bank. It is also mandatory that a hospital report to the Data Bank any disciplinary action taken against a physician in restricting or removing his or hers clinical privileges.

4. Each employee should be given a concise job description delineating precisely what his/her duties are.

5. Yearly evaluations of the employer's work should be made and discussed with the employee. Both positive and negative aspects of the employee's work should be described. A copy of the

evaluation should be placed in the personnel record and kept permanently.

6. The healthcare facility should have an active disciplinary process applicable to *all* employees. Discipline should be meted out fairly and uniformly.

7. Quality reviews should be held on a permanent basis for each of the health facilities clinical departments.

8. Whistleblowing should be welcomed and known as a policy by all employees of the facility.

9. Medical records should be up to date and reviewed for completeness and consistency.

CHAPTER III

OFFICERS AND DIRECTORS RESPONSIBILITY

Historically, non-profit hospitals were not considered to be liable for the negligent actions of physicians and other clinicians. This was firmly established in 1910 when a case in Maine (Jensen v. Maine Eye and Ear Infirmary, 107 Me 408, 78 Atl. 898) the judge indicated "that no principle of law seems better established than that which declares that a purely charitable institution cannot be made liable for damages for the negligent acts of its employees. 'Were it not so,' declared the court, 'charitable institutions of all kinds would ultimately cease or become greatly impaired in their usefulness.' "[1]

This concept of charitable immunity began to change in the 1950's. An author stated in 1952 that "formerly, there was some disinclination to take action against philanthropic institutions, but this attitude is disappearing. To a greater extent, charitable institutions are being held responsible by the courts."[2] Many of the original decisions exempting hospitals were based upon the belief that hospitals were inanimate organizations and thus could not practice medicine. Only physicians, it was concluded, could do so. This concept was eroded little by little until it finally disappeared in 1965

[1] Hayt, Emanuel, Hayt, Lillian R. and Groeschel, August H; Law of Hospital, Physician and Patient. Berwyn, Physicians Record Co., 1972, Page 283.

[2] Sloan, Raymond P. This Hospital Business of Ours. N.Y., G.P. Putnam's Sons, 1952. Page 54.

when the Illinois Supreme Court ruled in the case of Darling v. Charleston Community Memorial Hospital (33 Ill., 2d 326, 211 N.E. 2d 253, 14 A.L.R. 3rd 860 (1965), cert. denied, 383 U.S. 946 (1966)).

Highlights of the State Supreme Court decision in this landmark case are:

> "This action was brought on behalf of Dorrence Darling II, a minor... by his father and next friend, to recover damages for allegedly negligent medical and hospital treatment which necessitated the amputation of his right leg below the knee. The action was commenced against the Charleston Community Memorial Hospital and Dr. John R. Alexander, but prior to trial the action was dismissed as to Dr. Alexander, pursuant to a covenant not to sue. The jury returned a verdict against the hospital in the sum of $150,000. This amount was reduced by $40,000, the amount of the settlement with the doctor. The judgment in favor of the plaintiff in the sum of $110,000 was affirmed on appeal...
>
> "On November 5, 1960, the plaintiff, who was 18 years old, broke his leg while playing in a college football game. He was taken to the emergency room at the defendant hospital where Dr. Alexander, who was on emergency call that day, treated him. Dr. Alexander, with the assistance of hospital personnel, applied traction and placed the leg in a plaster cast. A heat cradle was applied to dry the cast. Not long after the application of the cast plaintiff was in great pain and his toes, which protruded from the cast, became swollen and dark in color. They eventually became insensitive. On the evening of November 6, Dr. Alexander 'notched' the cast around the toes, and on the afternoon of the next day he cut the cast approximately three inches up from the foot. On November 8 he split the sides of the cast... in the course of cutting the cast the plaintiff's leg was cut on both sides. Blood and other seepage were observed by the nurses and others, and there was a stench in the room... The plaintiff remained in Charleston Hospital until November 19, when he was transferred to Barnes Hospital in St. Louis and placed under the care of Dr. Fred Reynolds, head of orthopedic surgery at Washington University School of Medicine and Barnes Hospital. Dr. Reynolds found that the fractured leg contained a considerable amount of dead tissue which in his opinion resulted from interference with

the circulation of blood in the limb caused by swelling or hemorrhaging of the leg against the constriction of the cast. Dr. Reynolds performed several operations in a futile attempt to save the leg but ultimately it had to be amputated eight inches below the knee...

"The plaintiff contends that it established that the defendant was negligent in permitting Dr. Alexander to do orthopedic work of the kind required in this case, and not requiring him to review his operative procedures to bring them up to date; in failing, through its medical staff, to exercise adequate supervision over the case, especially since Dr. Alexander had been placed on emergency duty by the hospital, and in not requiring consultation, particularly after complications had developed. Plaintiff contends also that in a case which developed as this one did, it was the duty of the nurses to watch the protruding toes constantly for changes of color, temperature and movement, and to check circulation every ten to twenty minutes, whereas the proof showed that these things were done only a few times a day. Plaintiff argues that it was the duty of the hospital staff to see that these procedures were followed, and that either the nurses were derelict in failing to report developments in the case to the hospital administrator, or he was derelict in bringing them to the attention of the medical staff, or the staff was negligent in failing to take action. Defendant is a licensed and accredited hospital, and the plaintiff contends that the licensing regulations, accreditation standards, and its own bylaws define the hospital's duty, and that an infraction of them imposes liability for the resulting injury.

"The defendant's position is stated in the following excerpts from its brief: 'It is a fundamental rule of law that only an individual properly educated and licensed, and not a corporation, may practice medicine... Accordingly, a hospital is powerless under the law to forbid or command any act by a physician or surgeon in the practice of his profession...

" 'A hospital is not liable for the torts of its nurse committed while the nurse was but executing the orders of the patient's physician, unless such order is so obviously negligent as to lead any reasonable person to anticipate that substantial injury would result to the patient from the execution of such order... The extent of the duty of a hospital with respect to actual medical care of a professional nature such as is furnished by a physician is to use reasonable care in selecting medical doctors. When such care in the selection of the staff is accomplished, and nothing indicates that a physician so selected is incompetent or that such incompetence should have been discovered, more cannot be expected from the hospital administration.'

"The basic dispute, as posed by the parties, centers upon the duty that rested upon the defendant hospital. That dispute involves the effect to be given to evidence concerning the community standard of care and diligence, and also the effect to be given to hospital regulations adopted by the State Department of Public Health under the Hospital Licensing Act..., to the Standards for Hospital Accreditation of the American Hospital Association and to the bylaws of the defendant...

" 'The conception that the hospital does not undertake to treat the patient, does not undertake to act through its doctors and nurses, but undertakes instead simply to procure them to act upon their own responsibility, no longer reflects the fact. Present-day hospitals, as their manner of operation plainly demonstrates, do far more than furnish facilities for treatment. They regularly employ on a salary basis a large staff of physicians, nurses and interns (sic), as well as administrative and manual workers, and they charge patients for medical care and treatment, collecting for such services, if necessary, by legal action. Certainly, the person who avails himself of 'hospital facilities' expects that the hospital will attempt to cure him, not that its nurses or other employees (sic) will act on their own responsibility.'[3]

..."The Standards for Hospital Accreditation, the state licensing regulations and the defendant's bylaws demonstrate that the medical profession and other responsible authorities regard it as both desirable and feasible that a hospital assume certain responsibilities for the care of the patient...

"We believe that the jury verdict is supportable... On the basis of the evidence before it the jury could reasonably have concluded that the nurses did not test for circulation in the leg as frequently as necessary, that skilled nurses would have promptly recognized the conditions that signalled a dangerous impairment of circulation in the plaintiff's leg, and would have known that the condition would become irreversible in a matter of hours. At that point it became the nurses' duty to inform the attending physi-

[3] Here the court is quoting from the case of Bing v. Thunig (1957), 2NY2d 656, 163 NYS2d 3, 11, 143 NE2d 3, 8.

cian, and if he failed to act, to advise the hospital authorities so that appropriate action might be taken. As to consultation, there is no dispute that the hospital failed to review Dr. Alexander's work or require a consultation; the only issue is whether its failure to do so was negligence. On the evidence before it the jury could reasonably have found that it was...

"We agree that the doctrine of charitable immunity can no longer stand... a doctrine which limits the liability of charitable corporations to the amount of liability insurance that they see fit to carry permits them to determine whether or not they will be liable for their torts and the amount of that liability, if any. Whether or not particular assets of a charitable corporation are subject to exemption from execution in order to satisfy a judgment does not determine liability."

Thus, the hospital (and the hospital *is* the Board of Directors and because the Board invests its responsibilities to the Administrator, it includes the Administrator too) is responsible for *monitoring* the care that is given in the hospital. In order to do this the Board must review the credentials, background and recommendations of anyone applying for membership to the medical staff. The Board must also periodically review the activities of the staff prior to reappointment of them. It is the Board's duty to have competent staff.

As a result of the Darling case and of other similar cases the American Hospital Association has indicated that there are nine recognized functions of a hospital Board of trustees. These are:[4]

"1. Establish and maintain procedures for conducting the business of the board.

"2. Establish and update goals and policies for the hospital.

"3. Develop and continuously update a long-range plan for the hospital and ensure that decisions are made in accordance with that plan.

"4. Monitor and evaluate plans and programs to ensure that they meet hospital goals and policies and the objectives of the long-range plan.

---

[4] Hospital Trustee Development Program. Chicago, American Hospital Association, 1979, pages 6-8.

"5. Ensure the hospital's long-range financial stability.
"6. Select the CEO, define his duties and responsibilities, and evaluate his performance.
"7. Approve selection of medical staff and ensure that it is properly organized.
"8. Provide a process for evaluation of all phases of hospital performance, including the quality of medical care.
"9. Ensure the community is well informed about the goals and performance of the hospital; ensure that the hospital is meeting the community's needs."

It is an absolute duty of the Board of Directors to select competent administrative and medical staff and to not only monitor their activities but to evaluate the quality of care that the staff is rendering. How that evaluation is to be done must be established by the Board. The results of the evaluation should be available to the community. The Board is responsible for the total quality administration of all hospital activities. The Board is also entrusted to see that the needs of the community which the hospital serves are being met by the staff.

The Board has also been held responsible for the actions of its employees. This is the doctrine of respondeat superior which is discussed in detail in Chapter II.

As mentioned above the Board must supervise its medical, administrative and general staff. The responsibility to select competent staff is discussed in Chapter II. A number of courts, however, "have enunciated what has been called the doctrine of corporate responsibility, which recognizes the existence of a duty owed directly by a hospital to a patient in connection with the care and treatment given to him, and which accordingly holds that a hospital can be held liable for its own negligence in the absence of any negligence on the part of the treating physician...

"Although the concept of corporate responsibility has expanded the duty owed by a hospital in connection with the medical care and treatment rendered by a physician operating within its walls, the standard of care to which a hospital will be held in connection with reviewing of supervising treatment given by physicians, or in requiring consultation, remains the traditional standard of reasonable care in light of the apparent risk...

"Even in the absence of an employer-employee or principal-agent relationship between a negligent doctor and a hospital, liability has been imposed on a hospital on the theory of independent negligence in failing to review, supervise, or require consultation about the treatment given by the physician where the situation indicates that the hospital had the opportunity for such review but failed to exercise it, or that its servants were negligent in failing to call the attention of the proper hospital authorities to the improprietary or inadequacy of the treatment being given."5

The American Law Reports also indicates:[6]

"Whatever may have been the case in earlier times, it seems clear that as organized health care has developed, the hospital, as such, takes an increasingly active part in supplying and regulating the purely medical care which the patient receives. Much of the direct medical attention received by the patient is at the hands of staff members with whom he has made no direct contractual arrangement. Every doctor using the hospital facilities is ordinarily required to comply with its standards and subject his work to staff consultation, review, and regulation, at pain of losing his staff privileges, a loss which may effectively curtail his ability to practice his profession. And every doctor working in a hospital must to a large extent depend upon its laboratory and other technical facilities, and upon the services of its staff specialists and technicians, in order to effectively carry out his function.

"In view of these changes in the actual operation of hospitals and of the medical profession generally, it is not surprising that some of the earlier legal rules which tended to insulate hospitals from tort liability to patients in connection with improper or inadequate medical treatment rendered in the hospital have been called in question in some of the later decisions, with the result that in... Darling v. Charleston Community Memorial Hospital... the court has taken the position that a hospital may be held liable

---

[5] American Law Reports, ALR4th Cases and Annotations. Rochester, NY. The Lawyers Cooperative Publishing Co., 1982. Pages 61-2.

[6] Ibid. Volume 14. Page 878.

for the adverse effects of treatment approved by the doctor in charge, who was not an employee of the hospital, because of what was found to be its negligent failure to review his treatment."

"In some jurisdictions a hospital may be subject to the standard of care of the ordinarily reasonable man, rather than to the professional standard applied to doctors, and the proof of the requirements of this standard and of the failure of defendant to meet those requirements may perhaps be made otherwise than by the expert testimony of a member of the same profession, so that the obstacles of the widely noted 'conspiracy of silence' may be avoided... if it is true that hospitals do, under the modern practice, effectively guide and control the actions of the doctors using their facilities, it is almost inevitable that sooner or later, responsibility will follow this power.[7]

As mentioned earlier in this chapter one of the primary functions of a Board is to ensure the hospital's long range financial stability. This includes carrying out the fiduciary responsibilities of membership on a Board. In the case of Stern v. Lucy Webb Hayes National Training School for Deaconesses and Missionaries (381 Federal Supplement 1003 (1974) the fiduciary responsibilities of a hospital board were clearly outlined. In this case David Stern on behalf of his sons brought suit against the Sibley Hospital in Washington, D.C. alleging that the hospital had charged an excessive amount for services due to the fact that the trustees of the hospital had engaged in such improper activities as mismanagement and nonmanagement. Under the bylaws of the hospital the Board was to meet at least two times a year. In the interim an Executive Committee was to represent the Board and, according to the court's record, "was authorized... to open checking and savings accounts, approve the Hospital budget, renew mortgages and enter into contracts. A Finance Committee was created to review the budget and to report regularly on the amount of cash available for investment. Management of those investments was to be supervised by an Investment Committee which was to work closely with the Finance Committee...

"In fact, management of the Hospital from the early 1950's until 1968 was handled almost exclusively by two trustee officers... (who) were continuously involved on almost a daily basis

[7] Ibid. Page 879.

in the affairs of Sibley. They dominated the Board and its Executive Committee, which routinely accepted their recommendations and ratified their actions. Even more significantly, neither the Finance Committee nor the Investment Committee ever met or conducted business from the date of their creation until 1971."

The trustees testified that they approved all of the recommendations of the two and almost never bothered to read any of the hospital's audits or questioned the investments that were being made. Although, the court found no conspiracy on behalf of the members of the Board, they did find that the members involved themselves in mismanagement, nonmanagement and self dealing. What the court found has subsequently been the basis for what is expected from a member of a hospital board as related to that members fiduciary responsibilities:

"A director who fails to acquire the information necessary to supervise investment policy or consistently fails even to attend the meetings at which such policies are considered has violated his fiduciary duty to the corporation… While a director is, of course, permitted to rely upon the expertise of those to whom he has delegated investment responsibility, such reliance is a tool for interpreting the delegate's reports, not an excuse for dispensing with or ignoring such reports… A director whose failure to supervise permits negligent mismanagement by others to go unchecked has committed an independent wrong against the corporation."

In summation, the court declared the following:

"Each director or trustee of a charitable hospital… has a continuing fiduciary of loyalty and care in the management of the hospital's fiscal and investment affairs and acts in violation of that duty if:

"(1) he fails, while assigned to a particular committee of the Board having stated financial or investment responsibilities under the by-laws of the corporation, to use diligence in supervising and periodically inquiring into the actions of those officers, employees and outside experts to whom any duty to make day-by-day financial or investment decisions within such committee's responsibility has been assigned or delegated; or

"(2) he knowingly permits the hospital to enter into a business transaction with himself or with any corporation, partnership, or association in which he holds a position as trustee, director, partner, general manager, principal officer or substantial shareholder without previously having informed all persons charged with approving that transaction of his interest or position and of any significant facts known to him indicating that the transaction might not be in the best interests of the hospital; or

"(3) he actively participates in, except as required by the preceding paragraph, or votes in favor of a decision by the board or any committee or subcommittee thereof to transact business with himself or with any corporation, partnership or association in which he holds a position as trustee, director, partner, general manager, principal officer, or substantial shareholder; or

"(4) he fails to perform his duties honestly, in good faith, and with reasonable diligence and care."

It is not only the duty of a board member to attend meetings but it is absolutely necessary that he divulge a conflict of interest or an apparent conflict of interest to the rest of the members.

A hospital is, as shown in the Darling case, responsible for all the care rendered in the hospital. Another case clearly delineating this is Bivins v. Detroit Osteopathic Hospital (258 N.W. 2d 527). The court account is as follows:

"This case involves a malpractice action to recover damages for the death of James Bivins at 6:10 a.m., June 6, 1968, at defendant Detroit Osteopathic Hospital... The facts indicate that decedent entered the defendant hospital on May 28, 1968, for some tests. While in the hospital, an x-ray of Bivens' lungs was taken which showed a suspicious mass in the right lobe of the lung. Dr. Evans was called in for consultation. Dr. Evans examined the x-rays and determined that the only way he could get the difficulty diagnosed was by bronchoscopy...

"The operation was performed by Dr. Evans on June 5, 1968. While using a bronchoscope to perform the bronchoscopy, he performed a biopsy with cupped forceps in order to obtain some tissue and in doing so cut a vein in the right lung. This situation caused a massive amount of blood to fill the air sacs of Bivens' lungs. Dr. Evans then passed absorbent gauze down through the bronchoscope to stop the bleeding, and this procedure did stop the bleeding for the moment. Subsequent x-rays revealed that the air sacs were still filled with blood.

"Dr. Evans then performed a tracheotomy so an artificial respirator could provide the decedent with oxygen and so other equipment could be used to suction the blood out of the air passages in his lungs. Bivens died the following day from a lack of oxygen.

"Testimony... indicated that decedent was returned to his hospital room between 7:30 and 8:00 p.m. and that Dr. Evans left orders for the suctioning of blood from decedent's lungs. Suction was performed at 9:00 p.m. and a large amount of blood was removed. Another suctioning occurred at 12 midnight and then none after that point...

"Between 12 midnight and 6 a.m., hospital night interns and medical residents were present and could have assisted decedent. Hospital records do not show any call to a thoracic surgeon, but do indicate that no doctor or thoracic surgeon saw decedent between midnight and 6 a.m....

"The proper standard of care expected of a hospital staff toward hospital patients is such reasonable care and attention for their safety as their mental and physical condition may require... Hospitals are liable for want of ordinary care toward their patients... The amount of care required varies according to the particular circumstances...

"Expert testimony in the... case included testimony... that various members of the defendant hospital's staff administered and prescribed various drugs for decedent... (and that) the drugs aggravated decedent's condition by making his breathing more difficult. Evidence also exists that, despite his failing condition, decedent was left alone for a considerable period of time and that suctioning ordered by Dr. Evans was actually done only twice before decedent's death...

"We thus believe that a sufficient basis exists for the jury's finding of negligence on the part of defendant hospital.

"Hospitals have certain standards of care, similar to those of physicians and nurses, that they must meet with their patients, and ordinary negligence in treatment of patient is breach of that standard."

Hospital boards of directors, therefore, are also responsible for the actions of all the staff of the hospital, not just the physicians.

In summary we can best quote from American Law Reports:[8]

> "The directors of a corporation are bound to use due care and to be diligent in respect of the management and administration of the affairs of the corporation and in the use or preservation of its property and assets; for a breach or neglect of duty in such regard, they are liable for the losses or injuries proximately resulting...
>
> "It is generally agreed that what constitutes a lack of 'due care' on the part of a director depends upon the facts of the particular case, and it has been said that yesterday's standards of vigilence are inadequate today...
>
> "As to the measure of a director's duty in order to avoid liability for allegedly having failed to exercise 'due care,' some courts have said that he must have exercised that care which a prudent man would have exercised under similar circumstances, while others have said that he must have exercised that care which a prudent man would have exercised in the conduct of his own affairs...
>
> Among the rules announced, the court established the standard that corporate directors must exercise ordinary care and prudence, and that this includes the duty of reasonable supervision of officers and employees... Directors ought not to be shielded from liability for ignorance of mismanagement or defalcations by such officers and employees if their ignorance was the result of a want of that ordinary care the court had just required of them 'if that ignorance is the result of gross inattention.'...
>
> "The necessity of adequate supervision on the part of directors has become increasingly apparent in recent times... With respect to what constitutes 'proper supervision' on the part of corporate directors, there are several factors which have been almost invariably held to establish negligence of directors for which they will be held liable, if such negligence was the proximate cause of loss. These are failure on the part of directors to heed warnings of mismanagement or defalcations by officers and employees and to take action appropriate to the situation, a failure to adopt prac-

[8] Ibid, Volume 25, 1969, Pages 951-54.

tices and follow procedures generally accepted as necessary by the directors of other similar corporations, and an attitude of general indifference to corporate affairs."

CHAPTER IV

MEDICAL STAFF

In Michigan, in 1986, it was noted that a hospital, generally speaking, is not vicariously liable for the negligence of a physician who is an independent contractor and merely uses the hospital to treat his patients (Sassen v Community Hospital Foundation, 159 Michigan App. 231, 1986). Thus, the hospital cannot be held directly responsible for the acts of physicians who are not employees.

In the same year, it was pointed out that physiciasns have been found to be the agent of a hospital thus creating vicarious liability in the hospital for the physician's malpractice, where the plaintiff, at the time of his admission to the hospital, was looking to the hospital for treatment by medical personnel who were ostensibly agents of the hospital, rather than merely as the place where his physician would treat him. One relevant factor in this determination was whether the hospital provided the plaintiff with a physician or if there was a physician-plaintiff relationship independent of the hospital setting (Sassen v. Community Hospital Foundation, 159 Michigan App 231, 1986).

The critical question was whether the patient looked to the hospital for treatment or merely viewed the hospital as a place where his physician would treat the patient (Hinkelman v. Borgess Medical Center, 157 Michigan App 314, 1987).

In another case, in 1989, it was noted that the factors to consider in relation to malpractice are whether the individual had an independent relationship with the physician prior to entering the hospital and whether the hospital was really the site for treatment by the individual's own physician (Brackens v. Detroit Osteopathic Hospital, 174 Michigan App 290, 1989).

The period of limitation of actions against hospitals for malpractice is two years in Michigan.

In 1989, it was stressed that retention and supervision of staff doctors is an action for malpractice and is subject to the two-year malpractice period of limitation (Bronson v. Sisters of Mercy Health Corporation, 175 Michigan App, 1989).

In 1990, it was further added that claims for medical malpractice (and hospital) must be brought within two years after the last treatment of the defendant or within six months of the discovery of the malpractice claim (MCL 600.5804, 1990, Carr v. Wittingen).[1]

A precedent-setting case was brought to court in 1978. This case, Grewe v. Mt. Clemens Hospital, involved a man with a dislocated shoulder who was improperly treated in the emergency room of the hospital by an internal medicine resident. The doctor was not found guilty but the hospital was found guilty because he was its agent (Grewe v. Mt. Clemens Hospital, 404 Michigan App 240, December, 1978). It was stressed that there was no record of any preexisting patient-physician relationship with any of the medical personnel who treated the patient at the hospital. In fact, the internist did not even see the plaintiff until approximately 12 hours after he had been admitted to the hospital.

A 1986 amendment to Michigan laws paraphrased the laws and stated that government hospitals do not have governmental immunity except for hospitals operated by the Departments of Mental Health and Corrections. The latter departments enjoy full immunity in the operations of their hospitals. This statute was cited by the Supreme Court in Hyde v. University of Michigan Board of Regents, 126 Michigan App 233, 1986.

Hospitals act through agents such as nurses. Where both hospital and nurse are sued and a settlement is reached with the defendant nurse, a release also acts to release the hospital. (Theophelis v. Lansing General Hospital, 430 Michigan App 473, 1988). Expert

[1] It differs in regards to children.

testimony is required to establish a standard of care (Gallagher v. Detroit Macomb Hospital Association, 171 Michigan App 761, 1988).

In 1981 it was stressed that binding arbitration is the only remedy available for settlement of malpractice disputes between a patient and a health care provider, where an arbitration agreement has been properly executed and not revoked by the patient within 60 days of execution (Brown v. Siang, 107 Michigan App 91, 1981).

Liability for torts in medical practice have been analyzed in various cases that came before the courts. For example, in 1979 it was noted that a hospital has the duty to adequately staff the hospital to care for its patients and such duty applies to a hospital emergency room notwithstanding the absence of establishing hospital-patient relationships prior to the treatment of emergency room patients (Hamburger v. Henry Ford Hospital, 91 Michigan App 580, 1979).

A few years later, it was ruled that a child born with a genetic disease has no cause of action against a hospital arising out of the failure to inform the child's mother of the consequences of being a carrier of that genetic trait. There exists in Michigan no action for 'wrongful life' (Dorlin v. Providence Hospital, 118 Michigan App 831, 1982).

In other analyses of malpractice, it was mentioned that liability of the hospital or the physician exists where a patient suffers a heart attack or the like while undergoing unrelated medical procedures (17 ALR 3rd 796, 1982, Michigan).

Further, there is a liability of the hospital or medical practitioner under the doctrine of strict liability and tort or breach of warranty for harm caused by a drug, a medical instrument, or a similar device used in treating a patient (54 ALR 3rd 258, 1982, Michigan).

There is a liability of the hospital or a similar institution for giving an erroneous notification of the patient's death (77 ALR 3rd, Michigan). Also, the hospital is liable for a patient's injury of death as a result of a fall from a bed (9 ALR 4th, Michigan).

Finally, the hospital's liability for negligence in failing to review or supervise the treatment given by a doctor or to require consultation is presented in 12 ALR 4th 57, Michigan.

There have also been several decisions involving the standard of care. In 1979, in the Hamburger v. Henry Ford Hospital case (91 Michigan App 580, 1979), it was noted that the standards of care required by a hospital are similar to those of physicians and nurses and are breached by ordinary negligence in the treatment of a patient.

Three years later, in 1982, it was stated that a plaintiff alleges an action for medical malpractice against the hospital where the crux of his complaint is that the staff of the defendant hospital misdiagnosed his injury, misinformed him, and breached the standard of care practiced in the medical community (Atkins v. Annapolis Hospital, 116 Michigan App 558, 1982).

An interesting decision was rendered in 1979. It indicated that a Good Samaritan status conferring immunity from ordinary negligence on volunteers who respond to an emergency within a hospital does not alter a hospital's duty to adequately staff its emergency room, notwithstanding a lack of hospital-patient relationship resulting from emergency room procedures, there being nothing to indicate that the emergency room be treated differently under statute than other hospital departments (Hamburger v. Henry Ford Hospital, 91 Michigan App 580, 1979).

A year later a decision was rendered in regard to university hospitals. The court said that since the operation of a university hospital is more like the operation of a general hospital than a mental hospital, its purposes, planning and carrying out of activity, can be accomplished by other sources than government and thus is not protected by governmental immunity (Churchwell v. Board of Regents of University of Michigan, 97 Michigan App 163, 1980).

Another interesting case also involved Henry Ford Hospital in 1980. The court stated that in medical malpractice action, where the defendant physician was in charge of a surgical operation, an admission by another doctor that he cut in the wrong place would not relieve the defendant of responsibility, since the defendant had the duty to see that the operation was performed with due care (Orozco v. Henry Ford Hospital, 408 Michigan App 238, 1980).

A year later, it was stated that a hospital cannot be held liable for the actions of a physician who is an independent contractor, and merely uses the hospital's facilities to render treatment to his patients, absent of showing that the patient was led to believe that the contractor would act as the agent of the hospital (Wallace v. Garden City Osteopathic Hospital, 111 Michigan App 212, 1981).

Returning to the standard of care, we should like to point out that in the law books it is defined as the care that is generally recognized by practitioners as a proper treatment for the condition diagnosed. A description of "the standard of care" is found in medical books, not in law books, although there are Standard of Care statutes. The Michigan statute defines it as "the state of the art existing at the time of the alleged malpractice." In some cases, it is defined as "customary medical practice." It was also pointed out that the burden of proof is on the plaintiff to prove standard of care. It is absolutely required that the plaintiff present evidence in expert testimony that the defendant failed to meet the standard of care. Without such testimony the case must be dismissed. The defendant has no duty to defend until evidence of his alleged failure to meet the standard of care is presented.

We now come to a series of cases involving physicians and their relationships with hospitals and in which one of the authors was an expert witness. The cases illustrate the need for hospitals to properly credential its staff, to constantly observe the actions of its physicians, to be sure that the medical staff members are working within their proper classifications and are not exceeding the privileges that have been granted to them.

INTRODUCTION

D.C. was a marginally obese, black 36 year old female who was admitted to a Detroit hospital in August 1988. She had a two-year history of insulin-dependent diabetes and uterine fibroids.

In the beginning of August, the doctor who admitted her, assisted by another physician, performed a dilatation and curettage (D&C), a right salpingo-oophorectomy and total hysterectomy. During surgery, the doctor dissected the right ureter. Although he attempted to remedy the cut by suturing, he was unsuccessful. As a result of this surgery, Ms. C suffered the following problems:

- Post-operative anemia
- Right ureteral obstruction
- Right urinary extravasation and urinoma
- Drainage of urinary extravasation and urinoma
- Excision of necrotic ureter
- Paralytic ileus
- Right hydronephrosis

Specifically, the following chronology applies in this case:

Uterine fibroids diagnosed by ultrasound.

August 2	Admitted to the hospital for total abdominal hysterectomy
August 3	Surgery, including: D&C, right salpingo-oophorectomy, total hysterectomy and packing of the right infundibulopelvic ligament. A salpingo-oophorectomy was done due to the finding during the hysterectomy of a large cystic mass on the right ovary. During the retraction of the infundibulopelvic ligament, a hematoma was discovered and oversewn. It continued getting larger, so another doctor was consulted, intraoperatively. Deep locking stitches were used to obtain hemostasis.
August 9	Discharged.
August 18	Admission to the same hospital through the ER. Differential DX: right pyelonephritis v. right ureteral 1 obstruction.
August 19	IVP, by N.P., M.D.; was consistent with severe right ureteral obstruction. Also, finding of a mass-like density within the pelvic cavity, suggestive of hematoma or urinoma.
August 23	Left the hospital against advice, but on advice of another physician whom she had consulted. Admitted

	to another hospital within minutes of leaving first hospital.
August 24	High grade obstruction in the middle third of the right ureter was discovered.
August 24	Additional procedures performed: (1) right ureteral exploration; (2) drainage of urinary extravasation and urinoma; (3) excision of the necrotic ureter; (4) end-to-end ureteral ureterostomy. Post-op DX: right ureteral obstruction with one extravasation and urinoma formation.
September 6	Discharged. DX: (1) Right hydronephrosis secondary to iatrogenic injury to right ureter; (2) Diabetes mellitus; (3) Statue postoperative hysterectomy, right oophorectomy.

Standard of Care

In August of 1988, good and accepted hospital practice required that the authorities of this hospital do the following:

1. See that the patient is provided with competent medical and surgical care and treatment.

2. Constant observation of the surgical practices of physicians who are members of the staff as well as those who work in the Emergency Room.

3. In most hospitals the review of surgical privileges is an ongoing process. Usually privileges are reviewed every two years but in some hospitals this is done on an annual basis. The competence of the physician to perform certain operations is always considered and if there are any complaints which might indicate inabilities, the doctor is called before specific committees which have to do with his surgical privileges. We are also not aware if there were any specific complaints about Dr. B in the past, but we do know that he had difficulty walking and standing due to numbness in his feet, caused by diabetic neuropathy. Dr. B. was also said to have impaired vision due to glaucoma. In any case, it was incumbent upon

the hospital to observe their physicians and surgeons to be sure they could adequately carry out their functions in the care of patients.

Departures From the Standard of Care

The administrative staff of the hospital departed from good and accepted hospital practice in the following ways:

1. They failed to adequately supervise the work of Dr. B. in such a way that he would be limited in performing procedures, particularly those which might involve dissection of the right ureter.
2. Individuals coming into a hospital look to the hospital to provide them with medical treatment, and the hospital represents that medical treatment will be adequately performed by physicians who work in the hospital. Most hospitals do not simply furnish facilities for treatment, but are considered responsible for the work of its medical staff members and are required to set up standards in accordance with the Joint Commission on Accreditation of Health Care Organizations and other authorities, so that physicians would only be able to perform surgery and render treatment in accordance with their abilities. Apparently this hospital failed to adequately check the abilities of Dr. B. If so, this hospital seriously breached the standard of care.

Causations

Assuming Dr. B. had limited vision and a condition wherein his feet would periodically go numb, his condition may have led to the unnecessary dissection of the right ureter. This action led to a whole series of unnecessary surgery, pain and problems for D.C.

Obviously, the hospital involved in this case failed to properly supervise the actions of Dr. B., and did not realize that their failure could lead to very serious results in patients entering the hospital.

The next case involved a Mr. V.Z., who entered a hospital in the beginning of 1986 in Colorado Springs, Colorado.

A Brief Summary of the Facts

The following is a brief summary of the facts in this case. Mr. D.V.Z. is a 58-year-old white male who worked as an auto parts clerk until July 1984 when his place of employment went out of business. From then until January 1986, he was employed as a part-time worker at a family owned ice cream business. Mr. V.Z. had a history of heart problems dating back to 1979, when he underwent a triple bypass and a mitral valve replacement. The results of this surgery were excellent. In 1985, however, he began to have increased tiredness from physical activities.

On January 29, 1986, he underwent a heart catherization by Dr. S. There was an examination by Dr. J.A. on January 30 and it was noted that there was an increase in his pulmonary artery pressure. It was decided to proceed with the surgery.

He was admitted to the hospital on February 9, 1986, and underwent surgery involving the replacement of the mitral and aortic valves on February 10, 1986. It was performed by Dr. J.A. and assisted by Dr. J.R. with Dr. J.M. as anesthesiologist.

After surgery, D.V.Z. suffered poor left ventricular function which resulted in his being given Dopamine and Dobatamine for several days. He was transferred from the ICU to a regular ward on February 15 and continued to show gradual but progressive improvement.

There seems to be some indication that he had atrial fibrillation soon after surgery. When he was close to discharge for recuperation at home, it was decided by Dr. S. and Dr. A. that an electrical cardioversion was needed. The electrical cardioversion resulted in a slow heart rhythm with a respiratory and then a brief cardiac arrest. Although he was resuscitated rapidly from the event, he showed evidence of marked cerebral ischemia afterwards. He remained comatose for several days. He required ventilitary support for about 48 hours afterwards. He continued to require endotrachial intubation for control of secretions and had severe neurological deficits. He also had severe impairment of mental capabilities.

He was seen in consultation by a neurologist who recommended a neurological rehabilitation and consequently he was eventually discharged from the acute care unit of the hospital and transferred to the rehabilitation ward for further neurological rehabilitation. Eventually on the insistence of his wife, he was transferred to another hospital in Colorado Springs and after a rehabilitation program, he was discharged to home care with very limited functioning.

At present this patient remains in the family home, has limited functions, and has to be fed by a gastrostomy tube, has distorted or non-existent speech. There has been no improvement for some time.

This patient suffered global brain damage from cardiac arrest after a cardioversion to convert his normal sinus rhythm. The cardioversion was done because of atrial fibrillation (a fast heartbeat).

The cardioversion was not an emergency procedure, and could have been done at another time. It occurred 10 days after surgery, but a longer period could have elapsed. It was intended to lessen the chance of blood clots. At the time off the cardioversion a trained pulmonary technologist gave intubation and handled the airway. A trained CCU nurse was also present. The pulmonary specialist on the case was not present. The cardioversion was performed by Dr. S. and Dr. A.

Standards of Case

In February of 1986, good and accepted hospital practice in the field of primary care and internal medicine required that hospital authorities at the hospital in Colorado Springs do certain things:

1. Analyze all the aspects involved in performing elective cardioversion before the procedure is actually performed, especially as there had been new developments for the patient, even though he had two previous cardioversion operations.

2. If it was determined that elective cardioversion was to be performed before discharge from the hospital, such cardioversion should have been performed with a pulmonary specialist present, considering the aggravated condition of the patient following surgery 10 days previously.

3. Once the cardioversion was decided upon, a full consent of both patient and his spouse should have been secured.

4. The potential risks of anesthesia and the high energy electrocardioversion must be considered and adequate personnel to prevent any mishaps must be present.

Departures From the Standard of Care

1. The patient was still on oxygen when the cardioversion was started. The oxygen was actually reduced to one liter from two. There was also some reduction in the oxygen saturation level. The PH level was abnormal so that the patient was building up carbon dioxide, and may have been going into acidosis. The patient was getting only two liters of oxygen when he was wheeled into the unit. Normally, he should have been getting four.

2. Although a pulmonary specialist, Dr. W., was consulted prior to the cardioversion, he should have been present considering all the risks involved in this procedure.

3. There was a narrow opening in the patients' airway because of previous polio experience, and this complicated the situation.

4. Brevitol and Valium, which had been given previously, reduced the patient's respiration. Therefore, an anesthesiologist or an anesthetist should have been present at the cardioversion.

5. As the cardioversion was strictly an elective procedure, not one that was absolutely required by the patient's medical condition, it was necessary that an informed consent for the performance of the procedure be obtained.

Mrs. V.Z.'s objection, and the fact that the patient himself gave consent only a very short time before the procedure was performed, leads us to feel that informed consent was actually not secured. The patient was already under sedation when he gave consent.

The deviation from standard of care exists in the fact that an electrocardioversion calls for either a nurse anesthetist or anesthesiologist to be present. A nurse anesthetist is far more capable than a respiratory therapist in helping with endotrachial intervention and taking care of the patient, who requires special attention in regard to respiration. The patient had two previous cardioversions. This one was performed after some serious difficulties and complications following surgery 10 days previously. Previous cardioversions did not follow major heart surgery and were not performed at a time when the patient was under any kind of respiratory care or experiencing any respiratory difficulty.

It is the responsibility of the hospital to see to it that the standards of care which exist in similar situations are maintained. Regulations developed for surgery apply to all physicians who practice at a given hospital. The hospital and surgeons in this case deviated from accepted standards of care.

Causations

The failure to conform to good and acceptable hospital practice was the probable case of the injuries to D.V.Z., which included extensive brain damage caused by cardiac arrest, which may have been avoided.

It is more likely that Mr. V.Z.'s cardiac arrest was precipitated by oxygen deprivation which led to cerebral damage. It is also more likely than not, that had an anesthesiologist or pulmonary specialist been present at the time of the cardioversion, that he would have had a better chance of either not having brain damage, or much less brain damage than he has at this time.

Essentially this case involved the failure of the hospital to have an anesthesiologist or a pulmonary specialist at the time of the cardioversion. The fact that the hospital did not have either one present made them vulnerable to suit and had dire results as we have pointed out.

The next case involves the exceeding of privileges on the part of a surgeon in a small hospital in Wisconsin.

A Brief Summary of Facts

The following is a brief summary of facts in this case. Mrs. R.H. was a patient for ten days at B-Memorial Hospital in Wisconsin. During that time, Dr. T.P. performed two procedures - Endoscopic Retrograde Cholioangio-Pancreatogram (ERCP) and a Sphincterotomy. During the procedure Dr. P. made an unnecessary cut and intruded into the pancreatic duct. While this occurred a wire broke on the sphinctertome. In his deposition, Dr. P. said he saw a spark from the wire when it broke and the tip was in the pancreatic duct. Mrs. H. did not have pancreatitis before this procedure and he felt the situation definitely caused pancreatitis.

A fellow physician at the hospital, Dr. R., came in during the procedure, made some suggestions about the size of the cut, but did not stop Dr. P. in his surgery.

Later in May, 1986, Mrs. H. was transferred to the Mayo Clinic in Rochester, Minnesota, where she subsequently died.

Further facts should be pointed out. Dr. P. did not have privileges to do an ERCP or a sphincterotomy. He unsuccessfully attempted an ERCP in a different patient approximately one month prior to the incident involving Mrs. H.

The procedure involving Mrs. H. was scheduled one or two days prior to the procedure and was listed in the hospital's surgical log. It was not an emergency and Dr. P. in his deposition admitted that he did the sphincterotomy unnecessarily.

Furthermore, the primary treating physician for Mrs. H., Dr. H, for whom Dr. P. was a consultant, was the chief of the medical staff at the hospital and signed the reappointment for Dr. P.'s credentialing at the hospital. Dr. P. was not listed as having credentials to do ERCP or sphincterotomy and did not request this when he was admitted to hospital privileges in 1983, nor did he ever request it subsequently. The hospital had only one sphinctertome and the patient could have been transferred to another hospital, which is only about an hour away from this hospital.

The patient never signed a consent form for the procedure which was performed by Dr. P.

Dr. P. was on the staff of seven hospitals in all but had no privileges to do an ERCP or a sphincterotomy at any institution. He had never attempted a sphincterotomy at any time.

Dr. P. did not have any board certification. He failed the written portion of the Board for Internal Medicine in 1984.

It should also be pointed out that the hospital is a hospital of only 32 acute beds. Its average hospital census is 17 and it has 74 employees. It is not accredited according to the guide for the Health Care Field issued by AHA in 1989.

STANDARDS OF CARE

In May of 1986, good and accepted hospital practice in the field of Endoscopy required that the hospital authorities at this hospital do certain things:

1. Every physician must have approval for the surgery procedures that he performs. The doctor performed a procedure that was not permitted, and it was the responsibility of the hospital to stop the procedure or ask that he be assisted by another physician.
2. Make sure that every procedure is necessary.
3. Have the proper and sufficient equipment available for any procedure performed at the hospital. Make certain that the equipment is in working order.
4. Have the physician inform the patient before a procedure is carried out and secure a signed consent form after proper information is given to the patient on the procedure.
5. Transfer the patient to another hospital if there is more diagnostic equipment available at such a hospital and if the procedure could be performed with less risk at such a hospital.

DEPARTURES FROM THE STANDARD OF CARE

The hospital personnel and physicians at this hospital in Wisconsin departed from good and accepted hospital practice in the following ways:

1. Dr. P. did not have credentials to perform an ERCP or a sphincterotomy at this hospital, and since the procedure was scheduled at least two days before it was performed, he could have easily been asked to step aside or have the patient transferred to another hospital. It was agreed that it was not an emergency and that it might have been performed elsewhere. Dr. P. in his deposition admitted that he never performed a sphincterotomy. He admitted that he performed only one ERCP prior to this procedure and that he was not qualified to perform this procedure as he had failed his written examination for Board certification in Internal Medicine. He also admitted that he made an unnecessary cut that intruded into the pancreatic duct instead of a common duct. He also admitted that he could have transferred the patient to another hospital.

2. It was up to the hospital to make sure that every procedure was necessary. Dr. P. admitted that this procedure performed was unnecessary and that it really should have been preceded by another procedure, a cholongram. The surgery was declined by another physician but Dr. P. did not find out why the surgeon declined to do the procedure.

3. This hospital had an obligation to have the proper and sufficient equipment to do any procedure at the hospital. A sphinctertome comes in different sizes, but only one size was available. Therefore, when a wire broke in the sphinctertome, it was impossible to substitute another one. Dr. P. stated that there was only one in the hospital because "it was cost effective."

4. Dr. P. admitted that the patient never signed a consent form and was not informed of the risks involved in this procedure. Dr. P. admitted that death was a risk. Diagnostic equipment was available in another hospital, where the patient could have been transferred.

Causations

The failure to conform to good and accepted hospital practice was certainly a contributing cause to the subsequent death of the patient.

A procedure was performed which was admittedly unnecessary. Equipment was used without a backup and things went wrong during the procedure. The patient had to be transferred to another hospital because of pancreatitis and it is more likely that the pancreatitis led to her death.

Apparently, this case involved surgery that was admittedly unnecessary. Equipment was used that didn't have a backup and the procedure did not work out. The patient subsequently died and a large settlement was made to the family.

Conclusion

Again, it is stressed that hospitals must watch what their doctors do in surgery, must not allow them to exceed their privileges, must insist that they have backup that can handle any emergency situation, and that patients who probably should not be treated in a particular hospital should be transferred to one that is better equipped to handle the case.

Another interesting case where credentialing was involved is that of Robert T., which involved an incident in July and August 1982. Specifically, a large hospital in the center of Detroit was in the process of purchasing a smaller hospital in the suburbs. While the negotiations were going on, an administrator was placed by the larger hospital in the smaller one to oversee operations and to make sure that things were done according to Michigan law and current practice. It was understood that the larger hospital was responsible for credentialing the physicians of the smaller hospital. The day-to-day operations were under the jurisdiction of the larger hospital. The receiver of the smaller hospital was only to sign checks and to meet weekly with the administrator of the central hospital. One of the physicians at the suburban hospital was permitted to do considerable surgery, including surgery which was much more than the "minor surgery and plastic surgery" for which he had credentials. This doctor, however, performed a radical mastectomy, rectal repairs, abdominal surgery and hernia repairs. The patient developed serious infections and became "gangrenous". After being brought back to surgery two more times, it was decide to transfer him to another hospital. He remained twenty-five days in the second hospital before he was able to be discharged to his home. Suit was brought against the major hospital as well as the doctor involved. In general, it was felt that the administrator of the suburban hospital was an employee of the central hospital, and had a duty to watch all patients in the hospital and be sure that doctors did not exceed their privileges.

There have been a number of cases in which doctors were not qualified to do surgery, but were permitted to proceed because they were in the process of becoming certified in their specialties. For example, there is a case in which the same physician (Dr. A.) exceeded his privileges at two hospitals.

This particular doctor was only board eligible in general surgery. He was licensed in 1976, took his boards in 1978 and only passed the first part. He said he was board eligible in plastic surgery, as he had been accepted for the examination in 1981, but did not take the examination in time. He did take the written part in 1986. He had been trained in hand surgery in 1978 and was able to get privileges at several hospitals, performing hand surgery, cosmetic surgery, and hair transplants. He had a series of cases which involved eliminating baldness by inserting hair plugs. This procedure had gone on since 1982 and was permitted in several major hospitals. Dr. A. had been warned in several instances and in writing that he must secure full plastic surgery boards in order to continue this work. He failed to secure such approval, but was permitted to continue, basically because the hospitals involved could not attract other surgeons with the proper qualifications. Moreover, there were a series of twelve to fourteen lawsuits against Dr. A. and the state licensing board had begun to investigate the matter. The larger hospital was upset because he had been sued so many times and failed to notify the hospital every time he was sued. Moreover, the hospital had no idea of settlements made by the insurance company until the insurance company stopped carrying insurance for this particular doctor.

In addition, the doctor was notoriously delinquent in completing his medical records, and was warned by several hospitals that this would not be tolerated. He would be six to eight months late in completing a record, and therefore the chart was often not reviewed by Utilization or Quality Assurance Committees or any other group in the hospital.

What is astonishing in these cases is that the doctor was not qualified nor certified in surgery, or in plastic surgery, despite his attempts to secure such certification since 1978. He was also placed on a provisional staff back in February of 1982 by one of the major hospitals and was told in a letter that there was strong consideration for removal of his privileges unless he attained board certification in his specialty. Yet, as of 1991, Dr. A. still was only on the provisional staff, had been placed on the delinquent chart list on thirty different occasions, and was being censured for attending less than the minimum required staff meetings. In 1993 he lost his Michigan license and moved out of state.

We have attempted to point out that hospitals have a responsibility to observe proper credentialing, and to be concerned about the privileges of members of their medical staff. Certainly, if a doctor is not certified, he or she might secure provisional privileges, but these have to be reviewed on a regular basis, at least annually or biannually and pressure placed upon the doctor to secure proper certification. If he or she fails to do so, it is incumbent upon the hospital to reduce his/her privileges accordingly.

Similarly, doctors cannot be permitted to do surgery in which they are not qualified, nor take on procedures in surgery without the assistance of a surgeon who can take over in case there is a problem.

CHAPTER V

WE ALL EXPECT HIGH QUALITY OF CARE

Standards of care can be defined as what a reasonable physician, nurse or a hospital would do under the same or similar circumstance. It is that which is established by custom or authority as a model, criterion, or rule for comparison of measurement. Consumers and patients, as well as their families, expect that health care will meet a perceived level of quality in terms of outcomes. They feel that they have a perceived right to receive health care in a non-negligent manner and expect that all providers are competent and will provide high quality care.

The legal profession points out that there is an obligation to avoid, on their part, frivolous claims, and "nuisance" suits.

Providers, on the other hand, have to balance their personal standards, patient expectations, peer standards, payor expectations, and the courts' interpretation of community standards of care. It is recognized that there is a need for effective peer review, and review by health care organizations to promote and improve the quality of care. This is shared by all interested groups and there is a perception of the importance of risk management and effective patient provider relations.

On the other hand, many purchasers and payors of health care have a perception that neither government nor providers are doing an adequate job of controlling quality. There is often an implication that government and providers should control quality. There is also a perception that the economic objective of reducing costs and utilization may contribute to reductions in quality, access, consumer dissatisfaction and increases in liability and risk.

There is also a perception by many that the objective of increasing enrollment in managed care systems may lead to revised standards of care which are economically determined. The implication is there would be a reduction in quality and an increase in liability and risk.

Liability insurers have a perception that different premium rates are tied to assumed insurance risks rather than to the competence of providers. Some may also have a perception that differential premium rates are unfairly based on categories of provider risks, rather than an experience or competence of individual providers.

In general, society has the right to recover damages for torts designed to foster the prevention of negligence or accidents. They also have a perception that public licensing boards and agencies are not adequately controlling quality and are not really doing their job surveying health care providers.

Finally, there is a general feeling by society that there is an inadequate, accessible supply of competent physicians and other health care personnel and health care facilities.

In reading about various cases, we get the impression that patient safety may become an issue without adequate medical treatment. The use of equipment and consideration of patient activities in the health care setting prior to or subsequent to treatment is a risk management function. In short, there are often cases which result from the lack of patient safety precautions.

An example is a case where the patient alleged that a medical center was negligent in leaving her unattended with only "an unsafe," wheel-equipped stool as seating. The stool rolled out from under the patient, resulting in a fall and fracture of her hip.

The facts are simple. The plaintiff, an 80-year-old woman, presented herself to the radiology department for a routine mammogram. At this particular medical center, there was only one x-ray room, containing an x-ray machine, a mobile mammogram machine, a chair, a table, and an examination stool. The stool in question rested on four, non-locking wheels, which allowed the stool to be moved at will.

The patient was briefly unattended in the room. When the technician returned, the patient indicated that she had attempted to sit on the stool, which rolled out from underneath her.

The plaintiff contended that she was not aware that the room contained a normal chair, and further that the stool provided the only place for her to sit.

In analyzing this case, we cannot help but comment that rollaway stools are used extensively throughout the health care environment. There have been reports of stools rolling out from underneath both patients and staff while in normal use. The use of these stools is indicated when a physician, nurse or technician needs to have mobility while examining a patient or conducting a procedure.

Because these stools may pose a safety risk, it is important that the patient be directed to a sturdy, non-mobile chair. Similarly, it is recommended that in those areas where medical examinations or procedures do not require the staff to be seated and mobile, a non-mobile stool be substituted. Although falls can never be entirely prevented, recognizing potential risks and minimizing the potential will reduce their occurrence.

Next we come to the case of a 64-year-old female who was a patient at a Detroit convalescent home from the end of 1985 until she was transferred to a hospital in September 1988. She was diagnosed as having Diabetes Melitus and Schizophrenia. Her guardian was her niece who lived in the general area. The patient had a long psychiatric history with a diagnosis of Schizophrenia with behavioral problems. She had periods of anxiety during her stay at the nursing home, but managed to attend many activities and to be able to function quite well without assistance by nursing personnel. She was independent in her ambulation and was able to sit and enjoy the activities at the home without difficulty. However, she did have problems from the very beginning of her stay. She had to be encouraged a great deal to attend activities. She had great difficulty in controlling her smoking, even stealing from the nursing station and being restricted in her smoking activities on many, many occasions. The record shows that from the beginning of her stay in 1985, until the end of 1988, she occasionally smoked in bed and had to be instructed to only smoke in designated areas. She was observed to have sores and cuts due to her smoking habit and was caught smoking in her room while lying in bed on a number of occasions. There were some attempts to leave the facility which resulted in the need to closely monitor her movements. However, she was well enough to leave on field trips according to her doctor.

Progress notes record a few references to schizophrenia and her attempts to try to stop smoking. She apparently had a considerable tremor in her hands, nervous anxiety, and insomnia, according to the record in the progress notes. She had problems with overweight and dentures about the same time.

A quarterly review in 1987 noted that it was necessary to monitor her diabetic condition, but saw no changes in this condition, and that she was frequently monitored for the need to smoke only in the day room. She was independent in all her activities in daily living. She complained that her doctors saw her only specifically on many occasions. She also had difficulties with a shaking hand and reactions to some medications. She took her insulin together with other drugs without any difficulty. She was a good eater, was hungry even at night, but was often nervous and a poor sleeper. She responded to Tylenol and requested medications often, but in general was independent in taking care of herself.

In March, 1986, she left go to a local hospital on her own, but was brought back without difficulty. Some agitation was noted at the time.

In May, 1986, she had a serious hand tremor, and attempts were made for her to give up smoking. In July, 1986, tremors were again noted as were her tendency to stay to herself and her need to be reminded to take her insulin for her diabetes.

In the months afterwards there were several attempts to leave and also to stop smoking. She did leave in April of 1987 and went to her niece's home, but she was returned the same day and had to be constantly watched. In June of 1987, she was found on a bus after she left the home and was returned. There were similar attempts in July and August of 1987, when she was returned by security.

In November of 1987, there was a strong tendency to overeat and many violations of her diet were noted throughout most of 1988.

On September 14, 1988, she walked out of the nursing home to smoke outside. Her dress caught on fire. She was severely burned with second degree burns and was rushed to the hospital and died a month later.

In September, 1988, good and accepted nursing home practice in the field of long-term care required that the authorities of this particular nursing home do certain things:

1. Institute controls so that a patient can only smoke in designated areas and under observation so that she could not burn herself or do bodily harm.

2. The nursing home should have taken much more initiative in trying to stop this patient from smoking, especially when she could not be constantly observed. The records indicate that there were many attempts to encourage her to engage in activities in daily living and apparently to enjoy life at the home, but no attempts were made to cease smoking except to stop it in prohibited areas. Yet there were many violations of her smoking in designated areas, many attempts to leave the home, and no encouragement to cease smoking. There was some past history of mild mental problems. The patient was alert, oriented, and able to follow directions, yet there seems to be no evidence of any attempt to control her smoking and certainly to control it in designated areas. She had a strong tremor and was constantly dropping things out of her right hand because of her shaking, and yet her movements were not controlled.

Quarterly reviews mentioned several needs to monitor her frequently for smoking only in the day room, and yet apparently this was not followed up.

The nursing staff at this home departed from good and accepted nursing home practice in the following way:

1. They failed to institute control of the smoking habits of this patient. They failed to have her under sufficient observation so that she could not burn herself. They obviously did not follow the many notices of social services and her physicians to monitor her so that she could not possibly burn herself. Many notes in the chart indicate that she wanted to leave and did so, but they did not follow through on the observations in regards to smoking.

From all indications in the records, this patient was alert and in control of her mental faculties in such a way that she could have been persuaded to cease smoking or to only smoke under observation or only in the day room. She had experienced difficulties in this area in the past and had been warned about it, but apparently the nursing staff did not follow through as noted in the incident which occurred in September, 1988.

2. Under the legal doctrine of respondeat superior (See Chapter I), the employer is responsible for the actions of his employees. In this instance, the nursing home must be considered responsible for the actions of its nurses aides, and the other personnel who were taking care of this patient. The fact that she severely burned herself indicates that they were not following proper controls and did not take the necessary precaution to avoid such an accident.

The key to preventing such a potential liability situation, is to recognize the problem quickly and to take action to correct it. Proper documentation of corrective action is also appropriate, as soon as possible following the corrective action, while details are clear in one's memory.

Let us now consider another case which also involves safety. The plaintiff alleged that there was a failure to keep the premises in safe condition, as evidenced by melted snow from the visitors' shoes in the elevator. She slipped and fell, receiving multiple injuries.

The plaintiff was a 59-year-old woman who was accompanying her granddaughter to the medical center for a scheduled clinic visit. There had been a significant snowfall on this February day and snow and ice were still present on the ground from the previous day. The plaintiff testified that she and her granddaughter arrived by cab at approximately 9 a.m. They entered the main entrance and proceeded to the elevators adjacent to the security desk. The plaintiff and her granddaughter testified that there was no water or debris on the elevator floor at that time. They continued to their clinic appointment, but upon checking in at the reception desk, they were told that they had made a mistake. Their appointment was, in fact, scheduled for the following day. They left the clinic and immediately entered the same elevator they had previously used. The grandmother slipped and fell due to standing water in the elevator.

The plaintiff testified that an individual, allegedly an employee, was also on the elevator and that the employee left the elevator immediately following the fall. The employee apparently contacted security regarding the incident. The plaintiff and her granddaughter traveled to the main floor, and were met by a security officer who offered his assistance. A wheelchair was provided and the plaintiff was accompanied to the Emergency Room for treatment. The security officer also called housekeeping to mop up the water in the elevator.

At the trial, the plaintiff's attorney attempted to convince the jury that the medical center was negligent in allowing water to accumulate on the elevator floor creating a hazardous condition for patients and visitors. The medical center, on the other hand, was able - through testimony of the Director of Building Services and the security officer - to establish that standard policy required all employees to inform maintenance and housekeeping of potential hazardous conditions. Standing water or loose debris on the floor were examples cited as hazardous conditions to be reported. Testimony from these personnel indicated that it would be impossible for a single department to continually monitor all areas of the medical center, and by utilizing the eyes of all employees, maintenance and housekeeping would be able to correct hazardous conditions properly.

The plaintiff was required to prove that the medical center had been on notice that the hazardous condition existed. Her attorney was unsuccessful in that proof because the water was present on the elevator floor for such a short time, and it was immediately cleaned up once it was discovered. After a short deliberation, the jury awarded its verdict of "no cause of action" in favor of the defendant that all employees are, in fact, risk managers who are responsible for maintaining the safety of the medical center for patients, visitors and employees. Prompt notification to the appropriate departments of potential risks or safety concerns increases our ability to provide a safe environment for all.

Every year thousands of claims and lawsuits are filed against hospitals and medical centers by visitors, patients and employees who claim to have been injured by negligent care of buildings or premises. Such liability cases are expensive to defend and often involve the elderly, who may become more severely debilitated following a fall. A safe environment for the public and employees has to be a constant risk management concern.

Failure to follow through on a suggestion from one department to a physician or a hospital may create significant liability for health care providers. Attention to detail and constant efforts to review published reports is a risk management technique for administrative and professional staff. We have in mind two cases. A brief summary of the facts in one case may assist us in our analysis.

In October, 1986, a female patient presented herself to her doctor with complaints of upper gastric bleeding. She was admitted to the hospital and a chest x-ray was ordered. Because she was so ill, the x-ray department sent up a portable x-ray unit. The portable chest x-ray was taken in October, 1986. The radiologist in his report indicated that a repeat x-ray should be conducted because a vague density was identified by him, inconclusive of a diagnosis. The attending doctor said he was aware of the report while the patient was still in the hospital.

One year later, the patient was diagnosed with lung cancer and ultimately died in February of 1989.

A number of questions arise as they relate to the administration of the doctor and the hospital. One question arises as to whether the hospital had proper rules and regulations regarding the follow up of x-rays to insure that physicians received a copy of the reports. Analysis indicates that the physicians received two copies, one at their office and the other in their mailbox at the hospital.

The question then arises as to whether there is a means of giving the radiologist the responsibility of follow-up on patients for a repeat x-ray when it is deemed necessary. The radiologist to whom we talked felt that this was not practical, and that about 8 percent of x-rays show a need for such follow up. But they have no right to require the ordering physician to reorder an x-ray if he fails to order a repeat x-ray.

The next question is whether the radiologist in this case had a responsibility to perform a repeat x-ray, given the rules and regulations in effect at the hospital in October of 1986. When we did some extensive questioning of the attending doctor and the radiologist, we find that the radiologist had no responsibility to perform a repeat x-ray and that which would be somewhat impractical, especially since the attending doctor felt that it was his decision at all times to manage the case and that no one else should interfere.

In view of this, we suggested that the hospital not be made a party in the suit and this was agreed to by the plaintiff's attorney.

We observed a number of cases in which it was indicated that accurate medical record documentation might have avoided additional liability issues for nurses and physicians.

We have in mind a case in which a patient alleged that a failure to keep siderails up and a failure to properly monitor her during a grand mal seizure caused injury and resulted in a serious liability suit. The patient fell from a stretcher and subsequently claimed that she suffered injury to her teeth.

The essential facts of the case are as follows: The plaintiff was a 35-year-old woman who came to a medical center emergency room with a history of having suffered a generalized seizure earlier that day. The triage nurse, in noting the plaintiff's history, indicated that during the plaintiff's seizure, her father attempted to place a spoon between her teeth and tongue. In the process, several of her front teeth were broken. The plaintiff's broken teeth were documented in the emergency room note.

A review of the nursing chart revealed a 7 p.m. nurse's note indicating the plaintiff was, "Resting comfortably in bed (with) both side rails up." However, the notation, "With both side rails up" appeared to have been written through a line drawn after the entry and "with" appeared to have been squeezed in after the fact. Subsequent documentation indicated that the patient fell from a stretcher following a visit to the bathroom and was observed to have suffered a grand mal seizure. The notes detail the medical response and state that during intubation, a tooth was dislodged.

It was later determined that the nurse who wrote the note had a habit of drawing a line from the end of each entry to the edge of the paper. Occasionally, if she realized she had forgotten to make a particular notation, she would insert words or sentences over or under the line. Unfortunately, in contrast to the wording of the note, the plaintiff asserted that the side rails were down. The appearance of the note gave the plaintiff a persuasive argument that the note was altered after the lawsuit was filed to protect both the nurse and the hospital against allegations of negligence. This entry assisted the plaintiff's claim against the hospital as the appearance of the chart was utilized to cast doubt on the accuracy of the record. However, the detailed notes regarding the plaintiff's pre-existing dental condition minimized the plaintiff's claim for injury to her teeth and consequent damages.

Erroneous notations in the medical record may be corrected either when the entry is made or at later date, but such corrections must be made with care. Mistakes discovered at the time of charting may be corrected by placing a line through the error and initialing it to indicate who corrected the record. Late entries should be noted as such and a brief statement should be inserted to indicate why the entry is late. Otherwise, any alteration of the record, whether an addition or deletion, may be suspect as a self-serving entry for the benefit of the writer and intended as a cover-up or misrepresentation.

Health care providers must be aware that attempts to change a medical record may result in disciplinary action by the hospital and may be considered fraudulent concealment by the courts. It is a breach of the law which could result in criminal as well as civil sanctions. Never alter a medical record in an attempt to support or defend your treatment. It will most certainly result in severe problems for you personally and professionally and may seriously compromise the defense of a medical malpractice action.

Attention to detail and constant efforts to proofread public reports is a risk management technique for administrative and professional staff.

Verbal communication problems may have possible adverse patient care consequences if additional confirmation as to understanding or directive is absent. Confirmation of patient identity requires more than just treating the person who responds to a name being called.

In an interesting case at a major medical center, a patient alleged he was given the wrong medication, resulting in a severe reaction which required hospitalization.

The patient was a 21-year-old male who was seen at one of the ambulatory centers for his weekly allergy injection. He was called by his full name, followed the nurse into the exam room, and received his shot. He experienced a severe anaphylactic reaction which required emergency treatment and an overnight hospital stay.

Subsequently it was discovered that the patient was given an injection and dose which had been prepared for another patient with the same name.

Failure to identify the right patient and adequately review the patient's history and existing drug allergies prior to administration of the dose may result in a potentially catastrophic, adverse reaction. There are several ways in which mediations may create patient injury and consequent liability. Administering the drug to the wrong patient, prescribing a drug without ruling out medical problems which may contradict its usage, prescribing a drug which interferes with or complicates the usage of another prescribed drug, and prescribing a drug to which the patient has a known or reasonably ascertained allergy can result in serious injury and liability. Dosage and mediation errors are frequently cited as having contributed to patient injury. Accurate communication from the physician to other members of the healthcare team is essential. A misplaced decimal point or garbled telephone order may contribute to patient injury or death. Physicians, nurses, pharmacists and others have a responsibility to ensure that they correctly order, record, dispense and administer patient medications.

Scientific and technological innovation has assisted in providing safer and more efficient methods of health care delivery. However, people continue to play a significant role in health care delivery which presents a risk of human error. The following case is an example of preventable error and its consequences.

This case involved a 53-year-old male patient, who had been seen on several occasions for a heart-related condition. Before the admission in question, the patient had been rushed to the emergency room after a myocardial infarction and subsequent cardiac arrest. He was resuscitated and placed in the cardiac care unit. He was eventually stabilized and underwent a cardiac catherization. Weeks later, he was discharged in good condition. Subsequently, the patient returned for a follow-up visit and voiced no complaints regarding his cardiac condition. However, he indicated that approximately one week after his cardiac catherization he had begun to experience right thigh numbness and right leg weakness. A neurological examination was performed which revealed decreased sensation in those areas. The patient was referred to neurology for further evaluation.

An EMG was performed which isolated the patient's problem to a certain area. As a result, the patient was admitted to the hospital for a myelogram. A day later, he was taken to the radiology procedure room where the myelogram was to be performed. He was placed on a special procedures table and positioned on his stomach.

The procedure was to be performed in a darkened room by a radiologist with assistance from a technician. The technician had set the table with all the necessary equipment, including two identical plastic cups, each containing a clear liquid. One cup contained a myelogram contrast media and the other alcohol for cleaning the skin. Also on the table were the needle, tube and stylus for the injection of the contrast media. The patient, a rather heavy individual, experienced claustrophobia while strapped in position on the table. He briefly began to hyperventilate and complained of chest pains. The radiologist inserted the needle between the second and third lumbar vertebrae and verified its placement in the fluid chamber.

The procedure required the technician to fill the tube with contrast media and hand it to the radiologist.

However, the technician momentarily left the room and the radiologist, sensing the need to act promptly, proceeded to the table and filled the tube. He returned to the patient, attached the tube to the needle, and began the injection. The radiologist injected approximately one to two cc's and moved to the fluoroscope to take the radiologic images. Approximately 10 seconds after the injection, when he failed to detect an image on the fluoroscope, the physician heard the patient complain of pain in his flanks and hips.

Immediately he realized he had drawn liquid from the wrong cup and had injected alcohol into the patient's spinal column. The physician attempted to aspirate the alcohol with little success. The patient was stabilized and returned to his room. He was numb from the mid-thoracic area to the soles of his feet. He and his family were informed of the unfortunate error and its consequence. The patient was subsequently discharged with good recovery from coronary artery by-pass surgery, but there was little hope for return of sensitivity in his lower extremities.

Risk prevention systems which provide checks and balances have been created as a result of cases similar to these. It has led to careful labeling of injectables, staining non-injectables with methylene blue, implementing a cross-check system or using different containers for toxic substances. These are examples of risk prevention protocols.

These protections are often adopted after an unfortunate event and may be too late to prevent some harm to patients. In areas where confusion or distration can lead to disastrous consequences, it is essential that systems are implemented to better identify and label pharmaceuticals and liquids.

Next we have a case involving a failure to administer a required test or to ask questions of a patient which might have led to an immunization and prevented some serious consequences afterwards.

This case involved a patient who came to a clinic owned by a hospital. She was pregnant, was examined, and was never tested, i.e. no titer was given for Rubella, therefore her immune status was never discovered. She had a child, and was still not tested nor immunized. She was discharged from the hospital without being immunized.

She returned for a 6-week post-partum check-up, and was still not tested and therefore, her immune status was still not known. She returned for the insertion of an IUD and was still not tested when that would have been a good time to test her and to immunize her since after the IUD was in place, she obviously would not have gotten pregnant.

Months later she returned to the clinic for the express purpose of having her IUD removed because "I want to get pregnant." The doctor who saw her then testified that he did not test her for immunity, nor did he even think of testing her for immunity, and the IUD was removed.

Two months later, she returned to the clinic in the family owned unit or emergency room, and was seen by a doctor. He examined her and thought that she had regular measles, (Roseola). He said that she didn't tell him she was pregnant. She, on the other hand, insists that she told the doctor she was pregnant, because she said that she knew when she was even fifteen minutes pregnant!

In any event, later in the year, when she finally got to see a regular doctor, he began to treat her for her prenatal care and his group delivered a baby severely impaired by Rubella syndrome.

The child was nine years old at the time of the lawsuit. She was deaf and had severe vision problems. Her vision was probably 1 over 200; she also had mentation problems and some problems with her long bones, as well as having a repair of a patent ductus.

The lawsuit concerned the appropriateness of the care that the mother received. We are also concerned about the proximate cause of that care and its effect on the child.

It is interesting to note that while the hospital which owned the clinic was sued, along with the clinic and the doctors involved at the beginning, subsequently the hospital was removed from the lawsuit. It was felt that the clinic and its physicians were basically responsible for the unfortunate incident and not the hospital. This is clearly a case of omission of a test and a treatment with some rather dire consequences.

It could have been prevented by the doctors setting up a routine examination of patients such as Mrs. M., which had to be followed very rigidly.

Basically, this case illustrates the need for following the standard of practice, in this case one developed by the American College of Obstetrics and Gynecology.

One hospital, whose risk management department and attorneys we interviewed, discussed their program on preventing the type of cases we have just illustrated. The attorneys stressed the need for better documentation, the development of plans in dealing with patients who have diagnoses or special problems which could lead to possible lawsuits. The need for informed consent was mentioned over and over again. The need for better relations with patients was discussed.

Essentially this hospital advocated the following:

1. Constant talks by employees with patients so that they could eliminate misunderstandings.
2. Better physician-patient relationships.
3. The avoidance of promises that cannot be kept.
4. The importance of documentation.

It was suggested that incidents be reconstructed and families told what happened, so that actions to avoid future difficulties could be taken.

Years ago we felt that problems would simply go away. Today, we recognize the need to review all loss experience, summarize actions to be taken in newsletters, meetings, and discussions with physicians and employees.

CHAPTER VI

PATIENT RIGHTS AND RESPONSIBILITIES

Patients in hospitals and nursing homes have certain rights which have been delineated by Congressional and state legislation. Patient rights have also been defined by the courts in suits brought by patients against institutional providers. This chapter will briefly review those rights.

As an example of rights assigned by the United States Government are those outlined in the Federal Health Insurance for the Aged Regulations of the Social Security Administration for Skilled Nursing Facilities.[1] The governing body of the nursing home is required by the regulation to establish a policy guaranteeing certain rights. These include that the patient:

(1) Is fully informed, as evidenced by the patients written acknowledgment, prior to or at the time of admission and during stay of these rights and of all rules and regulations governing patient conduct and responsibilities;

(2) Is fully informed, prior to or at the time of admission and during stay, of services available in the facility, and of related charges including any charges for services not covered under titles XVIII or XIX of the Social Security Act, or not covered by the facility's basic per diem rate;

---

[1] See Federal Register, 39: 35775-76, October 3, 1974, paragraph 405.1121 (k).

(3) Is fully informed, by a physician, of his medical condition unless medically contraindicated (as documented by a physician, in his medical record), and is afforded the opportunity to participate in the planning of his medical treatment and to refuse to participate in experimental research;

(4) Is transferred or discharged only for medical reasons, or for his welfare or that of other patients, or for nonpayment for his stay (except as prohibited by titles XVIII or XIX of the Social Security Act), and is given reasonable advance notice to ensure orderly transfer or discharge, and such actions are documented in his medical record;

(5) Is encouraged and assisted, throughout his period of stay, to exercise his rights as a patient and as a citizen, and to this end may voice any grievances and recommend changes in policies and services to facility staff and/or to outside representatives of his choice, free from restraint, interference, coercion, discrimination or reprisal;

(6) May manage his personal financial affairs, or is given at least a quarterly accounting of financial transactions made on his behalf should the facility accept his written declaration of this responsibility to the facility for any period of time in conformance with State law;

(7) Is free from mental and physical abuse, and free from chemical and (except in emergencies) physical restraints except as authorized in writing by a physician for a specified and limited period of time, or when necessary to protect the patient from injury or to others;

(8) Is assured of confidential treatment of his personal and medical records, and may approve or refuse their release to any individual outside the facility, except, in case of his transfer to another health care institution, or as required by law or third-party payment contract;

(9) Is treated with consideration, respect, and full recognition of his dignity and individuality, including privacy in treatment and in care for his personal needs;

(10) Is not required to perform services for the facility that are not included for therapeutic purposes in his plan of care;

(11) May associate and communicate privately with persons of his choice, and send and receive his personal mail unopened, unless medically contraindicated (as documented by his physician in his medical record);

(12) May meet with, and participate in activities of social, religious and community groups at his discretion, unless medically contraindicated (as documented by his physician in his medical record);

(13) May retain and use his personal clothing and possessions as space permits, unless to do so would infringe upon rights of other patients, and unless medically contraindicated (as documented by his physician in his medical record); and

(14) If married, is assured privacy for visits by his/her spouse; if both re inpatients in the facility, they are permitted to share a room, unless medically contraindicated (as documented by the attending physician in the medical record)."

States have adopted similar regulations as part of their public health codes. An example of such is the following from Michigan:[2]

PUBLIC HEALTH CODE §333.20201

333.20201 Policy describing and responsibilities of patients or residents; adoption; posting and distribution; contents; additional requirements; discharging; harassing, retaliating or discriminating against patient exercising protected right; exercise of rights by nursing home patient's representative; informing patient or resident of policy; designation of person to exercise rights and responsibilities; additional patients' rights.

Sec. 20201 (1) A health facility or agency which provides services directly to patients or residents and which is licensed under this article shall adopt a policy describing the rights and responsibilities of patients or residents admitted to the health facility or agency. Except for a licensed health maintenance organization

[2] Michigan Public Health Code, Act 368 of 1978, as amended. Par 333.20201, pp. 389-92.

which shall comply with section 21086, the policy shall be posted at a public place in the facility and shall be provided to each member of the facility staff. Patients or residents shall be treated in accordance with the policy.

(2) The policy describing the rights and responsibilities of patients or residents shall include as a minimum;

(a) A patient or resident will not be denied appropriate care on the basis of race, religion, color, national origin, sex, age, handicap, marital status, sexual preference, or source of payment.

(b) An individual who is or has been a patient or resident is entitled to inspect, or receive for a reasonable fee, a copy of his or her medical record upon request. A third party shall not be given a copy of the patient's or resident's medical record without prior authorization of the patient.

(c) A patient or resident is entitled to confidential treatment of personal and medical records, and may refuse their release to a person outside the facility except as required because of a transfer to another health care facility or as required by law or third party payment contract.

(d) A patient or resident is entitled to privacy, to the extent feasible, in treatment and in caring for personal needs with consideration, respect, and full recognition of his or her dignity and individuality.

(e) A patient or resident is entitled to receive adequate and appropriate care, and to receive, from the appropriate individual within the facility, information about his or her medical condition, proposed course of treatment, and prospects for recovery, in terms that the patient or resident can understand, unless medically contraindicated as documented by the attending physician in the medical record.

(f) A patient or resident is entitled to refuse treatment to the extent provided by law and to be informed of the consequences of that refusal. When a refusal of treatment prevents a health facility or its staff from providing appropriate care according to ethical and professional standards, the relationship with the patient or resident may be terminated upon reasonable notice.

(g) A patient or resident is entitled to exercise his or her rights as a patient or resident and as a citizen, and to this end may present grievances or recommend changes in policies and services on behalf of himself or herself or others to the facility staff, to governmental officials, or to another person of his or her choice within or outside the facility, free from restraint, interference, coercion, discrimination, or reprisal. A patient or resident is entitled to information about the facility's policies and procedures for initiation, review, and resolution of patient or resident complaints.

(h) A patient or resident is entitled to information concerning an experimental procedure proposed as a part of his or her care and shall have the right to refuse to participate in the experiment without jeopardizing his or her continuing care.

(i) A patient or resident is entitled to receive and examine an explanation of his or her bill regardless of the source of payment and to receive, upon request, information relating to financial assistance available through the facility.

(j) A patient or resident is entitled to know who is responsible for and who is providing his or her direct care, is entitled to receive information concerning his or her continuing health needs and alternatives for meeting those needs, and to be involved in his or her discharge planning if appropriate.

(k) A patient or resident is entitled to associate and have private communications and consultations with his or her physician, attorney, or any other person of his or her choice and to send and receive personal mail unopened on the same day it is received at the health facility or agency, unless medically contraindicated as documented by the attending physician in the medical record. A patient's or resident's civil and religious liberties, including the right to independent personal decisions and the right to knowledge of available choices, shall not be infringed and the facility shall encourage and assist in the fullest possible exercise of these rights. A patient or resident may meet with, and participate in, the activities of social, religious and community groups at his or her discretion, unless medically contraindicated as documented by the attending physician in the medical record.

(l) A patient or resident is entitled to be free from mental and physical abuse and from physical and chemical restraints, except those restraints authorized in writing by the attending physician for a specified and limited time or as are necessitated by an emergency to protect the patient or resident from injury to self or others, in which case the restraint may only be applied by a qualified professional who shall set forth in writing the circumstances requiring the use of restraints and who promptly report the action to the attending physician. In case of a chemical restraint a physician shall be consulted within 24 hours after the commencement of the restraint.

(m) A patient or resident is entitled to be free from performing services for the facility that are not included for therapeutic purposes in the plan of care.

(n) A patient or resident is entitled to information about the health facility rules and regulations affecting patient or resident care and conduct.

(3) The following additional requirements for the policy described in subsection (2) shall apply to licenses under parts 213 and 217:

(a) The policy shall be provided to each nursing home patient or home for the aged resident upon admission, and the staff of the facility shall be trained and involved in the implementation of the policy.

(b) Each nursing home patient may associate and communicate privately with persons of his or her choice. Reasonable, regular visiting hours, which shall be not less than 8 hours per day, and which shall take into consideration the special circumstances of each visitor, shall be established for patients to receive visitors. A patient may be visited by the patient's attorney or by representatives of the departments named in section 20156, during other than established visiting hours. Reasonable privacy shall be afforded for visitation of a patient who shares a room with another patient. Each patient shall have reasonable access to a telephone. A married nursing home patient or home for the aged resident is entitled to meet privately with his or her spouse in a room which assures privacy. If both spouses are residents in the same facility, they are entitled to share a room unless medically contraindicated and documented by the attending physician in the medical record.

(c) A nursing home patient or home for the aged resident is entitled to retain and use personal clothing and possessions as space permits, unless to do so would infringe upon the rights of other patients or residents, or unless medically contraindicated as documented by the attending physician in the medical record. Each nursing home patient or home for the aged resident shall be provided with reasonable space. At the request of a patient, a nursing home shall provide for the safekeeping of personal effects, funds, and other property of a patient in accordance with section 21767, except that a nursing home shall not be required to provide for the safekeeping of a property which would impose an unreasonable burden on the nursing home.

(d) A nursing home patient or home for the aged resident is entitled to the opportunity to participate in the planning of his or her medical treatment. A nursing home patient shall be fully informed by the attending physician of the patient's medical condition unless medically contraindicated as documented by a physician in the medical record. Each nursing home patient shall be afforded the opportunity to discharge himself or herself from the nursing home.

(e) A home for the aged resident may be transferred or discharged only for medical reasons, for his or her welfare or that of other residents, or for nonpayment of his or her stay, except as provided by title 18 or 19 of the Social Security Act, 42 U.S.C. 1395 to 1396k. A nursing home patient may be transferred or discharged only as provided in sections 21773 to 21777. A nursing home patient or home for the aged resident is entitled to be given reasonable advance notice to ensure orderly transfer or discharge. Those actions shall be documented in the medical record.

(f) A nursing home patient or home for the aged resident is entitled to be fully informed before or at the time of admission and during his or her stay of services available in the facility, and of the related charges including any charges for services not covered under title 18 or 19 of the Social Security Act, 42 U.S.C. 1395 to 1396k, or not covered by the facility's basic per diem rate. The statement of services provided by the facility shall be in writing and shall included those required to be offered on an as-needed basis.

(g) A nursing home patient or home for the aged resident is entitled to manage his or her own financial affairs, or to have at least a quarterly accounting of personal financial transactions undertaken in his or her behalf by the facility during a period of time the patient or resident has delegated those responsibilities to the facility. In addition, a patient or resident is entitled to receive each month from the facility an itemized statement setting forth the services paid for by or on behalf of the patient, and the services rendered by the facility. The admission of a patient to a nursing home does not confer on the nursing home or its owner, administrator, employees, or representatives the authority to manage, use or dispose of a patient's property.

(h) A nursing home patient or a person authorized by a patient in writing may inspect and copy the patient's personal and medical records. The records shall be made available for inspection and copying by the nursing home within a reasonable time, not exceeding 1 week, after receipt of a written request.

(i) If a nursing home patient desires treatment by a licensed member of the healing arts, the treatment shall be made available unless it is medically contraindicated, and the medical contraindication is justified in the patient's medical record by the attending physician.

(j) A nursing home patient has the right to have his or her parents, if a minor, or his or her spouse, next of kin, or patient's representative, if an adult, stay at the facility 24 hours a day if the patient is considered terminally ill by the physician responsible for the patient's care.

(k) Each nursing home patient shall be provided with meals which meet the recommended dietary allowances for that patient's age and sex and which may be modified according to special dietary needs or ability to chew.

(l) Each nursing home patient has the right to receive representatives of approved organizations as provided in section 21763.

States have also indicated that there are certain responsibilities that patients have. The Michigan Public Health Code outlines those of the nursing home patient;[3]

(1) A patient or resident is responsible for following the health facility rules and regulations affecting patient or resident care and conduct.

(2) A patient or resident is responsible for providing a complete and accurate medical history.

(3) A patient or resident is responsible for making it known whether he or she clearly comprehends a contemplated course of action and the things he or she is expected to do.

(4) A patient or resident is responsible for following the recommendations and advice prescribed in a course of treatment by the physician.

(5) A patient or resident is responsible for providing information about unexpected complications that arise in an expected course of treatment.

(6) A patient or resident is responsible for being considerate of the rights of other patients or residents and health facility personnel and property.

(7) A patient or resident is responsible for providing the health facility with accurate and timely information concerning his or her sources of payment and ability to meet financial obligations."

As the law requires that all patients entering a facility receive the listing of rights it is strongly suggested that they also receive the above list of responsibilities.

Let us now review a few of the court decisions concerning patient rights including the issues of false imprisonment, provision of interpreters, provision of care to a patient despite the absence of the patient's cooperation, the right to refuse treatment, AID's and clinician-patient sexual relationship.

[3] Ibid par 333.20202, page 392.

Right to Refuse to be Treated

"A patient's refusal to consent to medical treatment allegedly necessary to sustain the patient's life has also been upheld on the ground that the constitutionally guaranteed right to privacy encompasses a person's right to decline medical treatment."[4] (In these cases the Courts have allowed the refusal when the patient has been declared to be competent.) As "living wills" and the appointment of advocates becomes prevalent the right to refuse treatment will be recognized as a standard procedure in hospitals and nursing homes. The passage of the Patient Self Determination Act by Congress which took effect on December 1, 1991, has laid the groundwork for state surrogate acts and legalized advance directives in which a patient has directed, in writing, and while competent, who will serve as an advocate for him or her in case they become incompetent and cannot make decisions concerning their care, custody or treatment. Thus, the patient has the right to self determination of what care they will or will not receive. A typical Act is the Michigan Patient Self Determination Act which took effect in 1992. The Act requires that each health care facility notify each patient that is admitted of his or her rights under the Act. The notice is as follows:

Advance Directives

Preamble

Each patient/resident has the right to be fully informed in advance about his/her care and treatment and of treatment that may affect the patient's/resident's well-being.

Each patient/resident further has the right to participate in planning his/her care and treatment or changes in care and treat-

[4] American Law Reports, ALR 3d Cases and Annotations, Vol. 93, Rochester, NY, The Lawyers Cooperative Publishing Co., 1979, page 71.

ment, unless adjudicated incompetent or otherwise found to be incapacitated under State law.

In the State of Michigan, a person of sound mind may create an "advocate directive" appointing another individual, a "patient advocate" to make decisions concerning his/her care, custody and medical treatment in the event that the person is unable to participate in such decisions. At present, an advance directive is also known as a "durable power of attorney for health care" or a "patient advocate designation." Michigan's standards for appointing a patient advocate and for serving as a patient advocate are established by Public Act 312 of 1990, Michigan Compiled Laws (MCL) 700.496.

Patient/residents are not required to make patient advocate designations. They may express their care and treatment wishes in other ways. For example, some patients/residents may have chosen to write a "living will," which is a written statement of the patient's/resident's choices about medical treatment. Or, patients/residents may simply choose to make their wishes known orally to their family, friends and/or the facility. Living wills and oral or written statements, other than in a patient advocate designation, may not be legally binding on the facility. However, they may be helpful to the facility in deciding what treatment to give to the patient/resident, and the facility may choose to abide by such statements.

In the case of a patient/resident adjudicated incompetent under the laws of Michigan by a court of competent jurisdiction, the rights of the patient/resident are exercised by the person appointed under Michigan Law to act on the patient's/resident's behalf.

POLICY

The facility shall provide a consistent and orderly method of notifying patients/residents of their rights under Michigan law to make decisions concerning their medical care, including the right to accept or refuse medical treatment, and to formulate advance directives. The facility shall not, however, require a patient/resident to designate a patient advocate as a condition of providing, withholding, or withdrawing care, custody or medical treatment.

PROCEDURE

1. At the time each individual is admitted as a patient/resident, the patient/resident shall be provided with a copy of the "Michigan Notice to Patients" as required by the Patient Self Determination Act (PSDA).

2. The facility shall inquire of each patient/resident, at the time of admission and then periodically thereafter, whether or not the patient/resident has executed an advance directive, a living will, or has otherwise made his/her treatment wishes known. The facility shall document in the patient's/resident's clinical record whether or not the patient/resident has done so, and keep a copy of any such written document in the clinical record.

3. Each patient/resident shall be provided the opportunity to participate in the planning and acceptance of his/her own plan of care to the extent he/she is capable of being involved.

4. In the event the patient/resident becomes unable to participate in medical treatment decisions:

a. *Where the patient/resident has appointed a patient advocate,* and the patient/resident becomes unable to participate in his/her medical treatment decisions, the patient's/resident's inability to participate should be determined and documented in the clinical record by the attending physician and one other physician or licensed psychologist. Facility staff shall then follow the instructions of the patient's/resident's duly appointed patient advocate regarding the care, custody or medical treatment of the patient/resident, except as otherwise provided herein.

(1) Before following the instructions of the patient advocate, staff shall determine whether the instructions are within the authority granted by the patient designation document. If staff determines that the instructions are outside such authority they may (but shall not be obligated to) follow such instructions.

(2) Staff shall not be bound by the decision of a patient advocate under the following circumstances:

(a) Where staff has actual knowledge that the patient/resident has revoked the patient advocate designation, in a manner provided by state law;

(b) Where the patient advocate has instructed staff to withhold or withdraw treatment which would allow the patient/resident to die, and staff has actual knowledge that the patient/resident has not authorized the patient advocate to make such a decision;

(c) Where staff has knowledge that the patient advocate is not complying with the requirement for patient advocates established by State law.

(3) Staff shall not follow the instructions of a patient advocate to withhold or withdraw treatment from a pregnant patient/resident that would result in the pregnant patient's/resident's death.

b. *Where the patient/resident has not appointed a patient advocate and has no guardian,* and the patient/resident becomes unable to participate in his/her medical treatment decisions, the patient's/resident's inability to participate should be documented in the clinical record by the patient's/resident's attending physician and other caregivers. In such a case, the facility may look to a living will or other evidence of the patient's/resident's treatment wishes, to determine what treatment to provide or withhold for the patient/resident (consistent with sound medical and nursing practice), provided the patient's/resident's family, friends, and/or significant others agree on what treatment should be provided or withheld. If there is a disagreement as to the treatment to be provided or withheld, the facility may choose to seek direction from the probate court, including the appointment of a guardian.

Michigan Notice to Patients Required by the Patient Self Determination Act (PSDA)

Your Rights to Make Medical Treatment Decisions

We are giving you this material to tell you about your right to make your own decisions about your medical treatment. As a competent adult, you have the right to accept or refuse any medial treatment. "Competent" means you have the ability to understand your medical condition and the medical treatments for it, to weigh the possible benefits and risks of each such treatment and then to decide whether you want to accept treatment or not.

Who Decides What Treatment I Get?

As long as you are competent, you are the only person who can decide what medical treatment you want to accept or reject. You will be given information and advice about the pros and cons of different kinds of treatment and you can ask questions about your options. But only you can say "yes" or "no" to any treatment offered. You can say "no" even if the treatment you refuse might keep you alive longer and even if others want you to have it.

What If I'm In No Condition To Decide?

If you become unable to make your own decisions about medical care, decisions will have to be made for you. If you haven't given prior instructions, no one will know what you would want. There may be difficult questions: for instance, would you refuse treatment if you were unconscious and not likely to wake up? Would you refuse treatment if you were going to die soon no matter what? Would you want to receive any treatment your caregivers recommend? When your wishes are not known, your family or the courts may have to decide what to do.

What Can I Do Now To See That My Wishes Are Honored In The Future?

While you are competent, you can name someone to make medical treatment decisions for you should you ever be unable to make them for yourself. To be certain that the person you name has the legal right to make those decisions, you must fill out a form called either a durable power of attorney for health care or a Patient Advocate Designation. The person named in the form to make or carry out your decisions about treatment is called a Patient Advocate. You have the right to give your Patient Advocate, your caregivers and your family and friends written or spoken instructions about what medical treatment you want and don't want to receive.

Who Can Be My Patient Advocate?

You can choose anyone to be your Patient Advocate as long as the person is at least 18 years old. You can pick a family member or a friend or any other person you trust, but you should make sure that person is willing to serve by signing an acceptance form. It's a good idea to name a backup choice, too, just in case the first person is unwilling or unable to act when the time comes.

Where Can I Get A Patient Advocate Designation Form?

Many Michigan hospitals, health maintenance organizations, nursing homes, homes for the aged, hospices and home health care agencies make forms available to people free of charge. Many senior citizens' groups and church and civic groups do, too. You can also get a free form from various members of the Michigan legislature. Many lawyers also prepare Patient Advocate Designations for their clients. The forms aren't all alike. You should pick one which suits your situation the best.

How Do I Sign A Patient Advocate Designation Form So That It's Valid?

All you have to do is fill in the name of the advocate and sign the form in front of two witnesses. But that's not as simple as it sounds, because under this law some people *cannot* be your witnesses. Your spouse, parents, grandchildren, children and brothers or sisters, for example, cannot witness your signature. Neither can anyone else who could be your heir or who is named to receive something in your will, or who is any employee of a company that insures your life or health. Finally, the law disqualifies the person you name as your Patient Advocate, your doctors and all employees of the facility or agency providing health care to you from being a witness to your signature.

It is easier to make a Patient Advocate Designation before you become a patient or resident of a health care facility or agency. Friends or co-workers are often good people to ask to be witnesses, since they see you often and can, if necessary, swear that you acted voluntarily and were of sound mind when you made out the form.

Do I Have To Give My Patient Advocate Instructions?

No. A Patient Advocate Designation can be used to name your Patient Advocate, the person you want to make decisions for you. But written instructions are generally helpful to everybody involved. And, if you want your Patient Advocate to be able to refuse treatment and let you die, you have to say so specifically in the Patient Advocate Designation document itself. Any other instructions you have you can either write down or just tell your Patient Advocate. Either way, the Patient Advocate's job is to follow your instructions.

Can I Just Give Instructions And Not Name A Patient Advocate?

Yes, you can simply tell somebody, for example, your caregiver or your family and close friends, what your wishes are. Better yet, you can write what is called a "Living Will," which is a written statement of your choices about medical treatment. Even though there is not yet a state Living Will law, courts and health care providers still find Living Wills valuable. Those taking care of you will pay more attention to what you have written about your treatment choices, whether in a Patient Advocate Designation or Living Will, because they can be more confident they know what you would have wanted. Most doctors, hospitals and other health care providers will also pay attention to what you've said to others, especially your family, about medical treatment. But again, it's better for everyone involved if you write your wishes down.

Do I Have To Make A Decision Now About My Future Medical Treatment?

No. You don't have to fill out a Patient Advocate Designation or Living Will and you don't have to tell anybody your wishes about medical treatment. You will still get the medical treatment you choose now, while you are competent. If you become unable to make decisions, but you've made sure that your family and friends know what you would want, they will be able to follow your wishes. Without instructions from you, your family or friends and caregivers may still be able to agree how to proceed. If they don't however, a court may have to name a guardian to make decisions for you.

If I Make Decisions Now, Can I Change My Mind Later?

Yes. You can give new instructions in writing or orally. You can also change your mind about naming a Patient Advocate at all and cancel a Patient Advocate Designation at any time.

You should review your Patient Advocate Designation or Living Will at least once a year to make sure it still accurately states how you want to be treated and/or names the person you want to make decisions for you.

What Else Should I Think About?

Treatment decisions are difficult. We encourage you to think about them in advance and discuss them with your family, friends, advisors and caregivers. You can and should ask your facility or agency about their treatment policies and procedures to be sure you understand them and how they work.

If you want more information about a Patient Advocate Designation or Living Wills, or sample forms, please ask your caregivers for assistance. Many facilities and agencies have staff available who can answer your questions. Additional materials may be available from your state representatives or senator.

Many health care administrators in states without such acts or without living will statutes, fear that allowing the patient to refuse treatment will jeopardize them legally. Susan M. Wolf, an attorney, writing in the Hastings Center Report has indicated that such fear is ill founded. She states that[5] "many healthcare professionals, administrators, and even lawyers wrongly… maintain that a directive broader than the statute is without legal effect. They make the common mistake of believing that once the legislature has recognized one means of protecting individual rights, there are no other means…Judges have long… recognized that patients have a common-law right to be free of unwanted bodily invasions… In case after case, judges have declared that patients have a common-law right to refuse unwanted life-sustaining treatment. That right is not confined to the terminally ill, and applies to the refusal of all life-sustaining treatment modalities including artificial nutrition and hydration. Nor does a patient even need to express the refusal in writing. Oral expression of preference may be effective as well… Any oral or written declarations from the patient are relevant evidence, including treatment directives broader than or different from the state statute…

> "Thus any memorialization of the patient's treatment preferences has legal force. At the very least, it constitutes relevant evidence of the patient's wishes. It cannot be dismissed or ignored."[6]

Because these self determination acts are new as of this writing there are no cases that can be reported. There is no reason to believe, however, that the court decisions will be any different than those in the past that Wolf has mentioned above.

---

[5] Wolf, Susan M. "Honoring Broader Directives." Hastings Center Report, September-October, 1991, page 58.

[6] Ibid, page 59.

FALSE IMPRISONMENT

Hospital's and nursing homes cannot detain a competent patient against the patient's will. Typical of such cases are the two reported below:

> "The forcible detention of an elderly man in a nursing home in spite of his expressed desire to leave and his numerous attempts to escape amounted, the court held in the following case, to false imprisonment.
>
> "Describing false imprisonment as the direct restraint of a person's physical liberty without adequate legal justification, the court held in Big Town Nursing Home, Inc. v Newmark (1970, Tex Civ App 10th Dist) 461 SW2d 195, that there was sufficient evidence to support a finding that a 67-year-old man had been falsely imprisoned in a nursing home, in which he was kept against his will for 51 days. Three days after he was taken to the home by a nephew, the man attempted to leave, but was caught by employees of the home who forcibly returned him to the facility, where he was placed in a wing with persons who were senile, addicted to drugs and alcohol, and mentally disturbed. During the ensuing weeks he repeatedly asked the manager and assistant manager of the home to be permitted to leave, and he attempted to escape five or six times, but was caught and brought back against his will. Following his escape attempts, he was confined in what was termed a "restraint chair." In addition, during the period of his detention he was not allowed to use the telephone and his clothes were taken from him. Describing the actions of the nursing home's staff as being in utter disregard of the man's legal rights, inasmuch as there was no court order for his commitment and since the agreement for his admission stated that he was not to be kept against his will, the court said that the staff acted recklessly, willfully, and maliciously in unlawfully detaining him."[7]
>
> "In a number of cases hospital patients have alleged that they were falsely imprisoned by hospital authorities who, the patients claimed, expressly or impliedly refused to release them unless they paid their bills or arranged for payment… (T)he courts held

[7] Ob cit, 4ALR 4th 449, pages 450-51.

that detention under such circumstances constituted false imprisonment."[8]

PROVISION OF INTERPRETERS

The United States under the provisions of Section 504 of the Rehabilitation Act of 1973 requires, in part, that "no otherwise qualified handicapped individual in the United States... shall solely by reason of his handicap, be excluded from the participation in, be denied the benefits of, or be subjected to discrimination under any program or activity receiving Federal financial assistance."[9] In the case of United States of America v. Baylor University Medical Center (711 F. 2d 38; 564 F Supp 1495) suit was brought by the United States for a hospital to provide an interpreter for hearing-impaired patients. The Judge in the case reported the following:

> "This is an action brought by the United States to enforce the provisions of Section 504 of the Rehabilitation Act of 1973... On the basis of certain complaints it received, HHS seeks to investigate defendant Baylor University Medical Center (Baylor) to determine whether hearing-impaired patients are provided effective services at Baylor's facilities, in compliance with Section 504. Baylor has refused to allow HHS to investigate it, on the grounds that it is not a recipient of "Federal financial assistance" within the meaning of Section 504, and therefore is not required to comply with the provisions of that section...
>
> "The following summary of the facts pertinent to this case is culled from the set of stipulated facts to which the parties agreed...
>
> "Baylor is a medical facility which receives federal funds from Medicare and Medicaid as reimbursement for services rendered to patients covered by Medicare and Medicaid. In July, 1977, in accordance with Department of Health, Education and Welfare regulations, Baylor signed and filed an assurance of compliance with Section 504 in order to receive Medicare and Medicaid pay-

---

[8] Ibid, page 451.

[9] 29 U.S.C., par 794.

ments. In signing that assurance, however, Baylor did not concede that Medicare or Medicaid would constitute federal financial assistance such that it would require Baylor to comply with Section 504...

"On May 9, 1980, the first of three complaints from the same complainant was filed with the Regional Office of HHS in Dallas, Texas. It alleged that Baylor had refused to permit a hearing-impaired person, a patient at the hospital, access to sign language interpreter services which she had contracted for at her own expense and which she needed to communicate effectively with the hospital personnel...

"Baylor responded through counsel on June 20, 1980, stating that it refused to subject itself to any investigation by HHS due to its belief that it received no "Federal financial assistance" within the meaning of Section 504. HHS then notified Baylor of its position that Medicare payments are considered Federal financial assistance and indicated that other payments to Baylor constitute such assistance. Baylor, however, held to its position that HHS lacks jurisdiction to investigate under Section 504. On August 25, 1981, HHS referred the case to the Department of Justice for enforcement action. The complaint in this action was filed on March 23, 1982...

"In Baylor's motion it contends... that Baylor is not a "recipient" of Federal financial assistance as that term is defined in the relevant regulations; and... that neither Medicare nor Medicaid payments constitute "Federal financial assistance" within the meaning of Section 504 and 45 C.F.R. (par) 94.3(h)...

"For its part, the United States argues in its cross-motion... that Baylor is a "recipient" of federal financial assistance, and... that both Medicare and Medicaid constitute such assistance...

"The rights and duties conferred by Section 504 apply with respect to "any program or activity receiving Federal financial assistance."...

"The term "recipient" is defined in the regulations to include "any... institution, organization, or other entity... to which Federal financial assistance is extended directly or through another recipient,... by excluding the ultimate beneficiary of the assistance." ...Assuming arguendo for the moment that Medicare and Medicaid are forms of Federal financial assistance, it is clear that Baylor is an institution to which Federal assistance is extended, and further that it is not Baylor but rather eligible patients who are the ultimate beneficiaries of the assistance. Thus Baylor is a "recipient" of federal assistance, so long as Medicare or Medicaid constitute such assistance.

"The chief argument raised by Baylor is that neither Medicare nor Medicaid is "Federal financial assistance" within the meaning of Section 504, and more particularly, the applicable HHS regulations. Specifically, Baylor contends that the Medicare and Medicaid funding which it admittedly receives are "insurance-type payments" and are therefore exempt from the statute's coverage by reason of the "contract of insurance" exclusion contained in HHS regulation...

"In considering whether either of these programs constitute "Federal financial assistance," several preliminary observations may be made. First, it has been noted that Section 504, as a remedial statute, should be "broadly applied and liberally construed." ...Next, the discrimination prohibition language contained in Section 504 was expressly modeled after the equivalent language contained in Title VI of the Civil Rights Act, and Title IX of the Education Amendments of 1982, and consequently the case law developed under Title VI and Title IX may be referred to for guidance in explicating Section 504... In addition, this Court may take into account the interpretation which HHS has given the statutory language "Federal financial assistance" over the years for "a court may accord great weight to the longstanding interpretation placed on a statute by an agency charged with its administration."...

"With these principles in mind, there are several reasons supporting the conclusion that both Medicare and Medicaid are "Federal financial assistance" within the meaning of Section 504 and do not fall within the "contract of insurance" exclusion...

"For these reasons, and in light of the broad construction which must be given to Section 504, this Court concludes that Medicare and Medicaid constitute federal financial assistance within the meaning of that provision and the applicable regulations...

"(A) recipient of federal funding must comply with the statute's nondiscrimination provisions "when a discriminatory program is 'benefited' by Federal financial assistance or when a federally assisted program itself is infected by a discriminatory environment."...

"Baylor admits that its in-patient and emergency room services - the activities at its facility that HHS seeks to investigate - are paid for in part through Medicare and Medicaid. Since these activities are directly benefited by federal assistance, they are proper subject of HHS investigation...

"Despite Baylor's argument to the contrary, the right of HHS to investigate a complaint is not restricted when the patient-complainant is not a beneficiary of either of the federal assistance programs (i.e. Medicare or Medicaid) which serve as the basis for the recipient's obligation to comply with the statute. The "programs or activities" language in Section 504 refers to the programs or activities of the recipient of the federal funding; it does not refer to either the federal funding programs themselves, or to the ultimate beneficiaries of these programs. Consequently, HHS has the right to seek enforcement of Section 504 upon those programs or activities at Baylor which benefit from Medicare and Medicaid, without regard to whether a particular complainant is a direct beneficiary of one of these federal assistance programs...

"In conclusion, this Court is of the opinion that the Government's motion for summary judgment must be granted. There are no material issues of fact in this case. The United States seeks the right to investigate into Baylor's compliance with Section 504 in connection with the provision of effective services for hearing-impaired persons in Baylor's in-patient and emergency room services. The United States is entitled to make this investigation."

AID's

Patients have the right to be protected from exposure to diseases carried by their caregivers. A new body of law is being gathered as patients bring suit against hospitals, nursing homes and physicians concerning being exposed to AID's. The first case in the health care setting, which as of this writing was awaiting appeal, is that of Faya v Almaraz and Rossi v Almaraz.

A Baltimore judge dismissed the complaints of patients Faya and Rossi in May, 1991 against a surgeon who later died of AID's. They claimed damages because of their fear that they may have been exposed to the AID's virus. Circuit Court Judge Joseph H. Kaplan stated in his decision:

> "It is a basic tenet of tort law that the courts will award compensation for an injury caused by the wrongful act of another... This Court, as a matter of law, cannot allow recovery for... fear."

There was no compensable injury, according to the court, because there was no exchange of bodily fluids, and no reported transmission from surgeon to patient, and thus, no proof of exposure.[10]

Providing of Care to Noncooperative Patients

When an institution accepts a patient for care it has an obligation to either continue that care or make arrangements for the patient to receive care elsewhere. An unusual case emphasizing this obligation despite all odds is that of Payton v Weaver (131 Cal. App 3d 38). Excerpts from the Court's decision of April 26, 1982 follows:

> "Occasionally a case will challenge the ability of the law, and society, to cope effectively and sensitively with fundamental problems of human existence. This is such a case. Appellant, Brenda Payton, is a 35-year-old black woman who suffers from a permanent and irreversible loss of kidney function... To stay alive, she must subject herself to two or three times a week to hemodialysis...
>
> "Brenda has other difficulties. Unable to care for her children, she lives alone in a low-income housing project... subsisting on a $356 per month Social Security check. She has no family support; one brother is in prison and another is a mental patient. She confesses that she is a drug addict, having been addicted to heroin and barbiturates for over 15 years. She has alcohol problems, weight problems and, not surprisingly, emotional problems as well.

[10] "Faya v Almaraz and Rossi v Almaraz" AIDS Policy and Law 6(11): 2, June, 1991.

"Despite these difficulties Brenda appears from the record to be a marvelously sympathetic and articulate individual who in her lucid moments possesses a great sense of dignity and is intent upon preserving her independence and her integrity as a human being. At times, however, her behavior is such as to make extremely difficult the provision of medical care which she so desperately requires.

"The other principal figure in this case is respondent John C. Weaver, Jr., a physician specializing in kidney problems. He conducts his practice through respondent Biomedical Application of Oakland, Inc. (BMA), which operates an outpatient dialysis treatment unit on the premises of respondent Providence Hospital.

"Dr. Weaver began treating Brenda in 1975 when, after the birth of Brenda's twin daughters, her system rejected a transplanted kidney. He has been treating her ever since. To her, 'Dr. Weaver is and was and still is the man between me and death... other than God, I don't think of nobody higher than I do Dr. Weaver.'

"On December 12, 1978, Dr. Weaver sent Brenda a letter stating he would no longer permit her to be treated at BMA because of her 'persistent uncooperative and antisocial behavior over... more than... three years... her persistent refusal to adhere to reasonable constraints of hemodialysis, the dietary schedules and medical prescriptions... the use of barbiturates and other illicit drugs and because all of this resulted in disruption of our program at BMA."

"In the latter part of 1978, Brenda applied for admission to the regular dialysis treatment programs operated by respondents Alta Bates and Herrick Hospitals, and was refused.

"For several months, Dr. Weaver continued to provide Brenda with necessary dialysis on an emergency basis, through Providence. On April 23, 1979, he again notified her by letter that he would no longer treat her on an outpatient basis. This letter led to Brenda's filing of a petition for mandate to compel Dr. Weaver, BMA and Providence to continue to provide her with outpatient dialysis services. That litigation was settled by a stipulated order which called for continued treatment provided Brenda met certain conditions: that she kept all appointments at the scheduled time; that she refrain from use of alcohol and drugs; that she maintain prescribed dietary habits; and that she 'in all respects cooperate with those providing her care and abide by her physician's prescribed medical regime.' Later, a sixth stipulation was added: that Brenda would 'enter into and participate in good faith in regular psychotherapy and/or counseling.'

"Dr. Weaver and BMA continued treatment of Brenda as an outpatient pursuant to the stipulation, but on March 3, 1980, Dr. Weaver, contending that Brenda had failed to fulfill any part of the bargain, again notified her that treatment would be terminated. He provided her with a list of dialysis providers in San Francisco and the East Bay, and volunteered to work with her counsel to find alternative care.

"Brenda then instituted a second proceeding... (which) alleges that all respondents have 'wrongfully failed and refused and continue to fail and refuse to provide Petitioner with regular hemodialysis treatment and medical supervision as required by her chronic end-stage kidney condition.'; and, more specifically, that the refusal by Herrick and the Alta Bates to admit her as an outpatient to their dialysis treatment programs violated their obligations under Health and Safety Code Section 1317 to provide 'emergency' treatment...

"The trial court... found that Brenda had violated each and every condition which she had accepted as part of the stipulated order... (and that) she displayed in general 'gross non-cooperation with her treating physician, BMA... and Providence Hospital.'...

"There was evidence that Brenda would frequently appear for treatment late or at unscheduled times in a drugged or alcoholic condition, that she used profane and vulgar language, and that she had on occasion engaged in disruptive behavior, such as bothering other patients, cursing staff members with obscenities, screaming and demanding that the dialysis be turned off and that she be disconnected before her treatment was finished, pulling the dialysis needle from the connecting shunt in her leg causing blood to spew, and exposing her genitals in a lewd manner...

"While it has been said that 'a private hospital owes the public no duty to accept any patient not desired by it, and it is not necessary to assign any reason for its refusal to accept a patient for hospital service'...it is questionable whether a hospital which receives public funding under the Hill-Burton Act... and perhaps from other sources, can reasonable be said to be 'private' in that sense... Rather, where such a hospital contains a unique, or

> scarce, medical resource needed to preserve life, it is arguably in the nature of a 'public service enterprise,' and should not be permitted to withhold its services arbitrarily, or without reasonable cause...
>
> "And, while disruptive conduct on the part of a patient may constitute good cause for an individual hospital to refuse continued treatment, since it would be unfair to impose serious inconvenience upon a hospital simply because such a patient selected it, it may be that there exists a collective responsibility on the part of the providers of scarce health resources in a community, enforceable through equity, to share the burden of difficult patients over time, through an appropriately devised contingency plan."

The court then indicated that there appeared to be the alternative available to assure "that Brenda does not die from lack of treatment" except to require Dr. Weaver to continue treatment. Thus, even although the patient has the responsibility to follow the physicians regimen the court has found, in this case, that if the consequences of stopping treatment is death, and if the hospital is one that has the scarce resources, then it is the obligation of the hospital in the absence of a contingency plan involving similar facilities with similar resources, to continue to provide that care.

CONFIDENTIALITY

It has been a sine qua non of patient care since the time of Hippocrates that the patient is entitled to confidentiality of his diagnosis and treatment. The Hippocratic Oath states "and whatsoever I shall see or hear in the course of my profession, as well as outside my profession in my intercourse with men, if it be what should not be published abroad, I will never divulge, holding such things to be holy secrets."[11]

---

[11] Miller, Robert D. Problems in Hospital Law, Rockville, Aspen Publishers, Inc., 1986, page 294.

> "The primary rationale for confidentiality of patient information," according to Robert D. Miller,[12] "is to encourage candor by patients and their associates to optimize diagnosis and treatment. Confidentiality also respects the patient's privacy; people should not have to broadcast details of their bodily condition to obtain medical care. Confidentiality can also promote candor by those caring for the patient."

As an example of maintaining confidentiality, even under very trying circumstances, is the case of Pritchard, et al v. Swedish American Hospital (191 Ill. Appl 3d 383 138 Ill. Dec. 658). In this suit the plaintiffs brought action for medical malpractice against the hospital and a number of physicians alleging "failure to order proper tests and treatment, failure to obtain proper consultation with specialists, inadequate monitoring of... (the patient's) condition and several other allegations. The hospital was accused of negligently rendering hospital services, failing to intervene in the patient's care and allowing "Dr. Richard Runstrom to maintain hospital privileges."

In the course of the trial, according to the court record, "the hospital disclosed that Dr. Runstrom's staff privileges had been suspended on October 6, 1975, and reinstated on February 3, 1976. These privileges had been suspended a second time on October 25, 1984, and had not been reinstated." The reason for the suspension of the doctor's privileges was that he was being treated for mental conditions. However, the hospital refused to submit specific information concerning the medical care given to Dr. Runstrom as such information, it was felt, was confidential.

Under the State Mental Health and Developmental Disabilities Confidentiality Act it was noted that all "records and communications shall be confidential and shall not be disclosed except as provided in this Act... The 'records' and 'communications' made confidential under the Act refer to any communication made during or in connection with providing mental health or developmental disability services, any record kept in the course of providing such services, and any information which indicates that a person is a

---

[12] Ibid, page 293.

'recipient.' ...'Mental health or developmental disabilities services' include 'examination, diagnosis, evaluation, treatment, training, pharmaceuticals, aftercare, habilitation or rehabilitation.'... A 'recipient' is defined as a 'person who is receiving or has received mental health or developmental disabilities services.' ... The exceptions to the Act, allowing disclosure by court order are very narrow, and none of them apply here...

> "To meet the avowed statutory purpose of protecting the confidentiality of the records and communications of those receiving mental health services, the Act is premised on a general prohibition against the disclosure of such information, except where specifically provided for in the Act... The general prohibition against disclosure of recipient records and communications was enacted because:
>
> 'Presumably, the patient in psychotherapeutic treatment reveals the most private and secret aspects of his mind and soul. To casually allow public disclosure of such would desecrate any notion of an individual's right to privacy. At the same time, confidentiality is essential to the treatment process itself, which can be truly effective only when there is complete candor by the patient. Finally, confidentiality provides proper assurances and inducement for persons who need treatment to seek it...'
>
> "We conclude that the information sought... dealing with Dr. Runstrom's mental condition was privileged and not discoverable under the terms of the Act and that, therefore, the trial court erred in compelling disclosure of this information...
>
> "In creating the physician-patient privilege, the legislature recognizes that patients have a right to be free from the embarrassment and invasion of privacy that often accompany the disclosure of medical information."

Thus, it can be seen that even under the most trying circumstances, information concerning a patients care is to be kept confidential. This is particularly true of mental health care. Most hospitals keep the records of mental health care separate from the rest of a patients medical record in order to protect the information from being revealed if the general record is to be released.

CHAPTER VII

CONSENTS

Negligence may consist of the failure on the part of a hospital or attending physician to reasonably inform the patient and/or the family of risks or hazards which may follow the treatment and/or service contemplated by the hospital or attending physician.

By "reasonably informed" we mean that the information must have been given timely and in accordance with the accepted standard of practice among members of the profession with similar training and experience in the community or a similar community and in the particular specialty.

The primary purpose of securing informed consent before admission and performance of procedures is to protect responsible physicians, members of the hospital staff, and the hospital itself against claims of unauthorized procedures, and to concurrently protect the patient from unsanctioned acts. While expressed consent may be given either orally or by telegram or telephone, written consent is safest because there is less room for misunderstanding about the contemplated procedure. As a result, written consent will normally be secured on the proper consent form, especially as a follow-up to an oral, telephonic or telegraphic consent.

Complete documentation of informed consent conversations is an important defense element to substantiate the information presented to the patient and the family.

Complications and adverse outcomes are an unfortunate reality of the practice of medicine. The manner in which the physician and hospital respond to these problem often determines whether a patient pursues litigation. Although litigation is sometimes unavoidable, a good physician-patient relationship, coupled with appropriate crisis response, can often temper the demands of the patient. Patients are entitled to full and honest disclosure regarding treatment-related problems. The manner in which information is relayed may favorably affect the acceptance of a patient.

The written, informed consent of the patient or his/her legal representative must be obtained by administration and the primary attending physician for hospitalization, all surgical operations, for the administration of any general or spinal anesthesia, and for all diagnostic or therapeutic procedures attended by some substantial risk, except in a medical emergency.

A medical emergency refers to a situation in which a patient has suddenly been endangered to the extent that immediate action is necessary to preserve the life of a patient or prevent an impairment of the patient's health. The signature of the patient or a responsible party also serves as acceptance of financial responsibility for services rendered as a result of admission to the hospital.

We now must consider who may consent. Valid consent to the furnishing of hospital, medical and surgical care and treatment may properly be given by the following:

A. A mentally competent adult; emancipated minor; married minor; and minor in the military service.

As a general rule, consent to treat and informed consent issues regarding minor patients ought to be addressed to the minor's parents or legal guardian. In Michigan, as in most states, a minor is one who has not yet attained the age of majority - 18 years.

When minor patients come in as an inpatient, outpatient, or in an emergency setting, it is necessary for the physician and health care team to locate and speak in person to the minor patient's parent or guardian. In the optimum situation, the physician will have an opportunity to obtain consent to treat, discuss the treatment alternatives, and obtain whatever specific consents are required from the parent or guardian and fully document this process in the medical record.

The age of majority and consent, as noted, is usually 18 years. An emancipated minor, however, may consent to medical and surgical care. Emancipation occurs by filing a petition in probate court or by operation of law when the individual:

1. is validly married, or
2. reaches the age of 18, or
3. is on active duty with the United States Armed Services, or
4. is in the custody of a law enforcement agency and a parent or guardian cannot be promptly located; treatment of minors in custody is limited to routine, non-surgical care or to emergency care.

Certain facts and circumstances may indicate that a minor is mature and has established sufficient personal and economic independence to achieve de facto emancipation status. These situations are extremely rare and questions regarding such minors should be directed to an attorney.

B. A parent of an unemancipated minor or unmarried minor; or legal guardian appointed to manage said minor's affairs if he or she has no parent or if the parents have been deprived of the minor's custody or control by a court.

Where there had been separation or divorce, the term parent shall mean that parent which has physical custody of the minor.

C. An individual appointed by a court (legal guardian) to act for a mentally incompetent patient.

A copy of the court order naming the guardian must be attached to the chart.

D. A parent, married or unmarried, for treatment of his/her child, regardless of the age of the parent.

1. An unmarried parent living with his or her parents, and obviously unemancipated, may consent for treatment of his or her

child; however, the consent of the child's grandparents should also be secured, if possible.

2. If the unmarried parent is emancipated, his or her consent is valid for treatment of the child.

E. A spouse or nearest next-of-kin of a patient who is unconscious and unable to respond.

In the event the spouse or nearest next-of-kin cannot be contacted, the question of consent should be referred to the hospital administrator or risk management department or the legal department.

F. Females, under 18 years of age, who are or who profess to be pregnant, may consent to emergency treatment related to the pregnancy only.

1. If the pregnant minor is already in labor, assistance to the delivery should be given, even though parental consent cannot be obtained.

2. In the absence of written consent of the pregnant minor, the minor's consent would be implied from her voluntary submission to medical assistance at the hospital.

3. When the delivery is to be by means of cesarean section or labor is to be induced artificially, the written consent of the minor should be secured. Parental consent should also be secured, if possible, but if it cannot be obtained, treatment without consent should still be undertaken.

G. If there is a question whether consent of a parent(s) is required in view of the age, mental condition or emancipated status of the patient, or because of the non-availability of the parent or similar factors; or if the question of mental competency of an individual has arisen and judicial determination has not been made the question should be referred to the hospital administration, the risk management department or an attorney.

Now the question of obtaining the consent will be discussed.

A. The primary attending physician who is to perform or supervise a contemplated operation or procedure is responsible for obtaining the proper informed consent from the patient for the patient.

B. The primary attending physician will inform the patient or his legal representative of the nature of the operation and the risks involved before obtaining written consent on a "Consent to Operation," form available at all doctor's offices, on all nursing units, and in the admitting office (consent implies knowledge of risks and consequences involved. The extent to which such is to be disclosed to the patient or his legal representative is a matter of medical judgment).

C. The "Consent to Operation" form should be completed by the attending physician to indicate that the patient or his/her legal representative was consulted and his signature affixed thereto.

D. In the presence of a witness, who should be a third party, the patient or his/her legal representative should sign the form (and indicate relationship to the patient if appropriate), as will the witness.

(1) What constitutes a legal signature:

(a) A person's name written by himself or a mark, i.e., an "x", dot, dash or line, made in the presence of a witness is considered a legal signature.

(b) If the person responsible for giving consent is the patient and the medical condition of the patient prevents him/her from signing the signature, the words "Patient Unable to Sign" should be written on the Signature of Patient line and witnessed.

E. Inappropriate paragraphs of the "Consent to Operation" form should be eliminated by lining out and having the person giving consent "initial" the paragraphs deleted (qualifications to any paragraph should also be recorded and initialed).

F. A new "Consent to Operation" form must be signed with each readmission or when it is decided to perform a radically different operation or administers a substantially different treatment from that which consent was originally given.

G. Written consent should always be coordinated with proper patient identification before each procedure. In operative cases verification should always be made as follows:

1. By the floor nurse, before administering preoperative sedation.
2. By the operating room nurse, before admission of patient to the operating room.
3. By the anesthesiologist (or anesthetist) before administration of anesthesia.
4. By the attending surgeon, before initiation or operative procedure.

Telegraphic or Telephonic Consent

A. Telegraph or telephonic consent is applicable in those cases where the individual authorized to consent is unable to come to the hospital and the patient is unable to give valid consent.

B. In such cases the wording of the telegraphic or telephonic consent should be the same as found in paragraph 1 of the "Consent to Operation" form or as is found in the first paragraph of the consent on "Emergency Admission Record."

C. The individual authorized to give consent should be instructed to send a telegraphic consent, collect, to the admitting office.

Witnessing of Consent

A. Registered nurses, licensed practical nurses and desk clerks may witness the signing of "Consent to Operation" forms in all areas of the hospital.

Consent for Treatment in an Emergency Situation

A. In an emergency of any nature when treatment is required immediately to preserve the life of the patient, or prevent serious impairment of the patient's health, and it is impossible to obtain the consent for him, the required procedure may be undertaken without express consent.

B. There are three important requirements for the emergency to justify acting without consent:

1. There must be a threat to the life or health of the patient;
2. The threat must be an immediate one and under the circumstances there is insufficient time to obtain consent; and
3. The hospital and the responsible physician must use every effort to document in the medical record the medical need for proceeding with treatment without consent (the documentation should clearly indicate the immediacy of the threat to life or health and the nature and magnitude; why a valid consent could not be obtained from the patient or person legally authorized to consent for him; and that the procedure carried out was only that which was necessary to remove the immediate threat to the patient's life or health).

Refusal to Consent

A. An adult patient, an emancipated minor, and a married minor who is conscious and mentally competent, or the parent(s) of an unemancipated minor, have the legal right to refuse and may refuse to permit any medical or surgical procedure.

B. The refusal to consent must be honored whether the refusal is grounded upon a doubt that the contemplated procedure will be successful, a concern about the probable or possible results of such a procedure, fear, religious belief, or mere whim. However, in the case of a minor, when treatment is necessary to preserve life, i.e., blood transfusion for the child of a Jehovah witness, the hospital will petition the court for a decision. This petition is filed with the risk management department.

C. It is recommended that no elective procedure be performed in the face of the patient's refusal to consent. The hospital and the attending physician should render the best possible care under the circumstances and:

1. The patient should be counseled as to the effect of such action. The words "patient refuses to consent" should be written across the face of the "Consent to Operation" form and the signature of the witness affixed thereto.
2. A brief description of the circumstances should be documented in the medical record so that it is clear that the attending physician used due care in recommending the proper treatment for the patient.

D. In emergent cases where the patient or the parent(s) of an unemancipated minor has given express refusal to consent, but, it is nevertheless deemed essential according to medical judgment of the attending physician that treatment should be administered immediately to preserve life or prevent impairment of health, the matter should be promptly referred to the hospital administration before any treatment is rendered.

We should like to cite one interesting case which involved an improper consent. This case was that of a 58-year-old man, Mr. D.V., who lived in Colorado, and at the time of this incident, had undergone several hospitalizations for heart disease. He had undergone mitral valve replacement, with coronary bypass grafting in 1979, and had also had replacement of the mitral and aortic valves in 1986. He was in the hospital in March of 1986 and was ready to go home. There was no apparent neurological problems following surgery and the attending surgeon felt that an elective cardioversion should be performed because of persistent atrial fibrillation. He asked the consent of the wife because the patient was in fairly difficult condition, and the wife refused the cardioversion, feeling the husband could go home and would get better in time. Despite the refusal, the cardioversion was carried out the next day, after Mr. V.D. was asked for consent while under sedation. He supposedly told the doctor to do whatever he felt was needed, and never signed any forms. This was considered consent and the surgery proceeded. Following the second electric shock, the patient went into cardiac arrest and cardiopulmonary resuscitation had to be undertaken. The patient was stabilized, but he was never the same. He remained comatose for several days and had to be transferred to a nursing home where he had to receive rehabilitative therapies for months. He gradually regained the ability to follow commands and to speak to some extent, but he was never able to regain independence and ambulation, and was described as "moderately severely demented." He also remained incontinent, was able to stand only with assistance, and was unable to comprehend television shows.

It was felt that the surgeon had proceeded without adequate permission for surgery, and the surgeon, under deposition admitted that there was no emergency in the situation. Moreover, despite the fact that there was no emergency, no anesthesiologist was present as in previous surgeries, nor even a nurse anesthetist, it was felt that the whole procedure could have easily been delayed. In addition, a pulmonary specialist who had been active on the case was not even asked if he favored the cardioversion. The attending surgeon and his assistant proceeded as though it was an immediate emergency, even though both of them admitted that it was not.

Literature indicates that there are many other instances of implied consent or improper consent.

CHAPTER VIII

SPECIAL PROBLEMS

In this chapter, we will handle a series of problems that have confronted hospitals and nursing homes and home health agencies, which have led to lawsuits in the malpractice field.

Specifically, we will deal with the following groups of problems: Escapes, violations of confidentiality, product liabilities, exceeding the statute of limitations, and the failure to provide a safe working environment for employees and patients. We will use cases in which one of the authors was involved as an expert witness, and materials noted in legal documents as examples of these problems.

We start with an interesting example of an escape. Mr. A.B. was a 68-year-old patient in a Veterans Administration Nursing Home in the Midwest. It is operated by the U.S. Government. The long-term care unit of the Veterans Administration Hospital was located on the fourth floor of the hospital, and took care of about 45 long-term care patients.

Briefly, Mr. A.B. went to play bingo on the same floor as his bedroom at 6:30 p.m. He was dressed in regular clothes, and at 8:30 p.m. failed to return to his room. When the nurses checked the various beds they noted he was missing and immediately made rounds throughout the floor to find him. He had often been confused in the past, and had actually gone to sleep in the wrong bed from time to time. At 9:30 p.m., the nurses decided he was missing and called security. Security searched the entire fourth floor and could not find Mr. A.B. They reported this to the nurses, who took no action until 4:30 a.m., when they called the patient's son at his home. The son arrived soon afterward, went through the entire floor and, finding his father still missing, called the police.

At 8:30 a.m., while the son was still waiting on the nursing home floor, the police found the patient dead, frozen to death in the bitter February weather. The home was sued.

It was pointed out that institutions are required to secure their doors in such a way that an alarm would go off if anyone left. This would be heard at the nursing station. The VA home did not have such an alarm.

Institutions are required to check patients in their beds at certain hours. If he was missing at 9:30 p.m., he should have been found long before the next morning.

The patient was known to have been confused and disoriented as to time and place, and had mentioned at various times in the previous months that he wanted to go home. His wife was an invalid herself and could not take care of him, so the patient was left at the nursing home. He did not have any posey belt, no bedside rails up, and was not under any special observation. He had problems with his heart, was a diabetic, had arterial sclerosis, and angina. He might have had a chair-fast or bed-fast arrangement, as he was wandering quite often, in the wrong beds and onto the wrong floors. Actually he was allowed to do and go as he pleased, and he was dressed in such a way that he could leave the home quite easily. He was not in any hospital garb, nor under any extra observation. He could have been prevented from leaving, and could have easily been accompanied to his bingo game when he left the ward by a volunteer, or a member of the family, or a staff member.

Unfortunately, there was no band on his wrist or clothing to identify him as a confused or wandering patient, and according to his doctor he should have been checked at least every hour.

The nursing staff failed to call for more help after he was gone an hour and a half. There was no follow up by calling police or requesting outside search by a member of the family, and in fact there was no request for any assistance. If the proper procedures had been followed, he probably would have been found and his life saved.

The staffing might also be questioned. There were three nursing employees for thirty patients which was barely enough for this kind of floor.

As noted, there were no alarms on the door, and no T.V. monitoring of any of the doors. We also learned that the hospital itself had no "elopement" policy, which means that they had no policy of what to do when patients left the premises without permission. This was actually required by the Health Department later on, but not at the time the incident occurred.

THE ISSUE OF CONFIDENTIALITY

We next turn to another special problem. Health systems are expanding rapidly, and information on patient care and treatment is often transferred and exchanged by various health care providers. Moreover, electronic systems are now increasingly applied to patient information. As data systems are developed and put into effect, the potential for unauthorized access to confidential information is more apparent than in the past. More individuals now have access to patient-related information and this creates a greater potential for unauthorized access and release of such information. Consequently, employees must be aware of their positions of trust and the importance of ensuring confidentiality. Thus, we came across a case involving a patient admitted to a psychiatric floor, who subsequently insisted that there had been an unauthorized release of information to third parties. The patient claimed that, as a result, his employment status was in jeopardy and he was embarrassed and humiliated. The patient stated further that only his wife was aware that he had been hospitalized but that his supervisor had obtained information by talking to hospital employees. Coincidentally, the daughter of the patient's supervisor was a nurse on his floor. The patient stated that this nurse must have informed her father that this patient had been admitted which, in turn, was shared with his co-workers.

Fortunately, discussions with the nurse showed that she was aware of the importance of confidentiality and that she was not the source of the alleged breach. An investigation showed that the patient's supervisor had called the hospital seeking information, but only after the patient's wife told him her husband had entered the hospital. When he contacted the hospital, the patient's admission was confirmed, but no further information was released. No unauthorized discussions had taken place regarding this patient. Investigation revealed that the patient himself had made numerous telephone calls to various friends and co-workers while in the hospital. Consequently, the evidence was clear that there had been no breach of confidentiality by hospital employees. On the other hand, the patient personally waived the privilege through his own actions.

In a second case, the patient had undergone tests to rule out a viral infection. The patient's former girlfriend - who was employed by the system and was aware that the patient had visited a certain clinic - had the ability to access the computer to obtain laboratory results.

The patient later learned that members of his health club were aware of his health problems. They began to ask him questions regarding his diagnosis and prognosis. At the same time, the system employee was also a member of the same health club. The patient was later told that the employee was the source of information regarding his health. The patient then telephoned and registered a complaint regarding the unauthorized disclosure.

An investigation was made and it was indicated that the employee, overcome with curiosity, had obtained access to the computer database outside the scope of her job responsibility. She called up the patient's test results, and improperly disclosed patient-related information. The employee's actions were investigated and she admitted she had improperly accessed the database. She was appropriately counseled and disciplined.

All employees have to be aware of their responsibility to ensure they maintain the confidential nature of patient-related information. Disregard of such responsibility may result in significant disciplinary action. Various system-wide personnel policies address issues of this kind.

A major hospital in the Midwest has issued the following statement: "[The system] protects the legal rights of employees and patients against breach of confidentiality. Such information includes personnel and/or medical record data, wage information, and other confidential statements and/or materials. Divulging information regarding a patient or employee to an unauthorized third party, using confidential information for personal use, and/or removing confidential information from hospital premises is subject to disciplinary action up to and including immediate discharge."[1]

Employees have to recognize that patients are entitled to the same protection that they, as employees, are provided and that the credibility and liability of the entire system can be adversely affected by the compromise of such policies.

The best approach to reduce, if not eliminate, this risk is to exercise caution when addressing issues of patient care with fellow health care workers. Further, as use of computerized medical records increases in the health care field, more individuals will have ready access to patient information. All employees must be aware of the trust vested in them by virtue of their employment status and must carefully respect patients' rights to confidentiality.

Product Liability

Hospitals use vast and varied quantities of technical machinery and supplies. If these products and supplies are defective or malfunction, the hospital may be exposed to certain injuries which can result. Even though the hospital may not manufacture or sell such products, their use creates an exposure which must be managed. Although product failure may not result in patient injury, equipment problems must be reported to the proper departments in a facility, through unusual occurrence reporting systems. Timely reporting of such incidents is essential to prevent patient injuries. In addition to notifying the appropriate departments and filing re-

[1] Henry Ford Hospital, CAVEAT, Vol. 3, No. 5, May 1991, p. 2.

ports, care must be given to preserve the defective product or equipment.

If an injury does occur, it is of the utmost importance that the defective product or equipment is separated from those used on patients. A so-called "chain of evidence" must be preserved to protect the integrity of the product or equipment. Chain of evidence procedures limit the number of individuals who are authorized to handle or inspect the equipment following an incident. Documentation must be kept of all such activity. The purpose is to preserve or protect the equipment so that any allegations that the hospital lost, tampered or destroyed the equipment may be defeated. In addition, it is the goal of the hospital to determine whether the problem involved product defect or operator error. If the hospital had prior notice of potential problems with a product, or if improper usage of the product was a direct cause of the malfunction, the hospital may be liable for damages.

Moreover, the hospital is not the only party with a vested interest in protecting the evidence. The product manufacturer will likely want to inspect and test the equipment that is questioned. Certainly, it is in the manufacturer's best interest to rule out design defects or malfunction and establish that human error contributed to or caused the problem. Consequently, following an incident involving a product malfunction, manufacturer-initiated discussions and inquiries should be directed to the proper department in the hospital, whether it is the hospital attorney, or the administrator's office, or an office of medical legal affairs.

There have been recent changes to the Federal Food, Drug and Cosmetics Act which require hospitals and other providers, such as nursing homes and outpatient facilities, to file reports regarding injuries caused by the use of certain medical devices within a facility to the federal government. This legislation is entitled, "The Safe Medical Devices Act," and it took effect in November of 1991. The Act defines "device" as any instrument, apparatus, machine, implant or other similar article, which is intended for the use of diagnosis, treatment or prevention of disease. Excluded are instruments which achieve their primary therapeutic purpose through chemical action with the body. The hospital has to provide two types of reports: defective medical incident reports and semi-annual summaries. The first report is to be used when reporting the discovery of defective devices. The second, when reporting all of the defective medical devices during the previous six-month period. The Act provides that a hospital is required to report when there is a probability that a device caused or contributed to a patient's death and/or a serious illness or injury.

The Act defines "serious illness or injury" as one which is life threatening and results in permanent impairment of a bodily function, or which necessitates immediate medical or surgical intervention to preclude permanent impairment of a bodily function.

If a medical staff member or employee becomes aware of such circumstances, an incident report must be filed with the Secretary of Health and Human Services and the device manufacturer if the device causes the patient's death. If the device results in a serious illness or injury but not death, only a report to the manufacturer has to be filed. In the event of a serious illness or injury where the manufacturer is not known, a report should be sent to the Secretary. In each instance, the report must be filed within ten days after a facility becomes aware of the defective device.

The party preparing the report is protected against any civil action against the author of the report, or the facility, unless there is knowledge that the information is false. On the other hand, the Secretary of Health and Human Services may disclose the identity of the facility to the manufacturer of the device for purposes of enforcing the provisions of the Act. There are definite penalties for noncompliance.

The evidence must be preserved, which enables the cause of the malfunction to be determined and prevented from reoccurring. It also ensures that the equipment is not tampered with and, thus, protects its integrity in case of litigation.

It is felt that if these guidelines are followed, quality patient care is increased and a system-wide risk control effort is in place.

Now we would like to turn to a case involving defective products which relate to patient injury. This example illustrates the importance of prompt reporting by individuals involved in similar situations.

In this case, the patient's parents alleged a failure to properly monitor their infant daughter during an MRI study resulting in second-degree burns to her foot.

The premature infant had developed a tracheal stenosis. To determine the cause of this narrowing, an MRI study was ordered. The patient was given Pavalon, an anesthetic, as a sedative for the procedure.

When this MRI procedure is performed on adults, a probe, or gaiting device, is placed on the patient's finger to monitor pulse. This device shoots an infrared light, which measures the blood flow and synchronized heart rate, to obtain a clear and diagnostic picture. But, for an infant patient, the probe must be placed on the child's foot to obtain optimal monitoring results.

The probe was removed following completion of the MRI and a burn mark identical to the rectangular shape of the gaiting device was discovered on the top of the child's foot. During the procedure, the technicians did not notice any changes in the monitor signal which would have warned them that the equipment was not functioning properly. Since the child was sedated, there were no cries or other indications that the child was experiencing the burn.

There were several issues involved: whether the hospital was negligent and had not properly monitored the patient during the procedure; or whether the device was inherently defective; or whether the MRI operator made an error which caused a malfunction.

The staff involved in this incident were helpful in providing valuable information regarding the use of this device. In accordance with procedure, the device had been immediately removed from use following the incident. Inspections were conducted by both the manufacturer and the hospital, in the presence of a representative of the legal department. Important issues were considered and included the maintenance history of the device and whether or not it had been previously cited, inspected, or repaired for a similar problem. The MRI Department was able to produce inspection and maintenance records which helped establish and support the defense position that the hospital was not on notice of any potential problems arising from the use of this device. Since the legal department had established a chain of custody, preserved all evidence, and had the ability to produce complete maintenance records, this case developed in a strong defense posture. The resolution of the case reflected an equitable apportionment of the responsibility of each defendant and the case was resolved appropriately.

STATUTE OF LIMITATIONS

The plaintiff in this case, Mr. H.A., was injured on December 3, 1977, when he fell down the stairs in his house. He immediately sought treatment at a Detroit area hospital. He was discharged from the hospital on the same day after x-rays were taken and after being told by the hospital staff that he had not suffered any fractures. After being discharged he continued to experience pain. In January, 1978, he visited his physician who determined that he had suffered a fractured foot, probably from the December 3, 1977 fall. On January 21, 1980, the plaintiff filed an action against the hospital and others. The hospital's motion for accelerated judgment, claiming the suit was barred by the statute of limitations, was granted by the Wayne County Circuit Court. The plaintiff appealed, alleging an error in the application of the two-year statute of limitations for malpractice actions to his cause of action instead of the three-year statute of limitations for ordinary negligence. But the court held that the two-year limitations period was correctly applied to this action since a malpractice action was properly pleaded against the hospital.

The plaintiff's claim is one for medical malpractice since he alleged that the staff of the defendant hospital misdiagnosed his injuries, and then misinformed him.

The plaintiff's suit was not filed on a timely basis. His cause of action accrued when he was discharged from the hospital. He knew of acts or omissions by the staff of the hospital and had reason to suspect the treatment was improper after visiting his physician. Yet, he failed to file his suit within six months after he discovered, or after he should have discovered, his cause of action. The accelerated judgment was properly granted based on the plaintiff's failure to file suit within the six-month period provided for malpractice actions.

It should be pointed out that a two-year statute of limitations applies to a hospital when a cause of action for malpractice is properly placed against the hospital. The focal point in determining what period for limitation of actions controls in a particular case is the type of interest allegedly harmed.

The applicable period of limitations depends on the theory actually pled where the same set of facts can support either of two distinct causes of action.

A plaintiff alleges an action for medical malpractice against a hospital where the crux of his complaint is that the staff of the defendant hospital misdiagnosed his injury, misinformed him and breached the standard of care practiced in the medical community.

Medical malpractice is the failure of a member of the medical profession, employed to treat a patient professionally, to fulfill the duty to exercise that degree of skill, care, and diligence exercised by the members of the same profession, practicing in the same or similar locality, in light of the present state of medical science.

A two-year period of limitations for medical malpractice, rather than a three-year period for ordinary negligence, applies to a complaint presenting a standard of conduct issue which cannot be determined by common knowledge and experience, but rather, raises a question of medical judgment.

A medical malpractice action accrues at the time that the defendant discontinues treating the plaintiff in a professional capacity; the action must be commenced within six months after the plaintiff discovers, or should have discovered, his cause of action.

A plaintiff discovers a cause of action for medical malpractice when the act or omission of the defendant becomes known and the plaintiff has reason to believe that the medical treatment either was improper or was performed in an improper manner.

Another case in which the statute of limitations applied is a case of a 15-year-old patient named Valerie Johnson, who sued Children's Hospital of Michigan. Valerie was admitted to Children's Hospital in May of 1974, for treatment in connection with a congenital heart condition. During her treatment, an intravenous needle in her arm became dislodged, causing the medication to infiltrate the dorsum of her right hand. This caused an ulceration on her right hand, which eventually required a skin graft to be performed on the injured area. On March 27, 1977, Miss Johnson reached the age of maturity. On March 8, 1979, she filed a malpractice suit against Children's Hospital. A motion for entry of default was granted. The parties later stipulated to set aside the default, and the court so ordered. The defendant then filed an answer to the plaintiff's complaint and a motion for accelerated judgment. The trial court granted the motion for accelerated judgment on the grounds that the plaintiff's action was barred by the statute of limitations because her injury was complete in July of 1974, that she was aware of it at that time, and that she waited for more than a year after reaching the age of majority to bring the action. The plaintiff appealed. It was held as follows:

The propriety of the lower court's decision to grant accelerated judgment in favor of defendant turns upon which statute of limitations actually controls in the instant controversy. The action was brought as a malpractice action. The statute of limitations for malpractice is two years from the accrual of the cause of action. At the time that plaintiff's treatment was terminated, a cause of action for malpractice would accrue when treatment was discontinued or when the plaintiff, in the exercise of reasonable diligence, should have discovered the asserted malpractice, whichever was the last to occur. Plaintiff alleges that she did not discover the asserted malpractice until January of 1979, when she consulted her attorney and learned of the possibility of a cause of action for malpractice. Defendant contends that the malpractice statute of limitations is inapplicable because at the time that plaintiff terminated her treatment, the malpractice statute of limitations applied only to licensed professionals and not to nurses or hospitals. Defendant argues that the statute of limitations for a personal injury negligence action is the proper statute of limitations to apply in this case. That statute grants a plaintiff 3 years from accrual of the cause of action to bring suit. A cause of action under this statute would accrue when all of the elements of the cause of action had occurred and could be alleged in a proper complaint. In plaintiff's case, this would have occurred in June of 1974. Under this theory, even granting plaintiff the one-year grace period upon reaching the age of maturity, her action would be barred by the statute of limitations. Because plaintiff failed to allege the existence of an agency relationship between the defendant and its agents or employees, liability cannot be predicated on a theory of respondeat superior. If such a theory had been properly pled, the malpractice statute of limitations might possible have been applicable. Under the facts of this case, however, defendant's position as to the relevant statute of limitations appears to be correct. The trial court did not err in granting the defendant's motion for accelerated judgment. This was affirmed.

Safe Working Environment

It is incumbent upon hospitals and nursing homes to provide a safe working environment for the employee and the patient as well. We first want to cite the case of Hamburger vs. Henry Ford Hospital.[1] Dr. Albert Hamburger entered Henry Ford Hospital having symptoms consistent with a mild stroke. While on the x-ray table he collapsed, became unconscious and started urinating. One of the student trainees, functioning as an x-ray technician, called for help and four other hospital employees arrived. The doctor was lifted onto a stretcher. They failed to support his head and it struck a metal guard rail. An action was brought by Dr. Hamburger and his wife in the Wayne County Circuit Court, alleging that the blow on the head caused neurological deterioration. The defendant hospital claimed the blow was not the cause. Verdicts of substantial sums were issued for Dr. Hamburger and his wife by a jury. A judgment on the verdicts was issued and the defendant appealed raising two issues: 1) whether the trial court should have granted the defendant's motion for a new trial based on its trial objection to the misconduct of the plaintiff and of plaintiff's counsel who allegedly made verbal and facial responses while defense witnesses

[1] Hamburger vs. Henry Ford Hospital, Docket 78-3138, 58 Am Journal 2nd. New Trial #212, 213.

were on the witness stand, and 2) whether the defendant was entitled to an instruction on gross negligence based on the good samaritan statute.

It was held that the grant or denial of a new trial was within the sound judgment of the trial court. The trial judge was in a position to see the facial responses and verbal conduct and assess their impact on the jury and there was nothing in the record which would indicate an abuse of discretion.

The good samaritan statute excuses only physicians, nurses and specified hospital personnel from civil liability where volunteer assistance is performed in an emergency situation, without gross negligence or willful and wanton misconduct. A hospital, due to the high standard of care it is required to provide patients, may be held liable for ordinary negligence in the treatment of a patient by employees where a hospital-patient relationship exists at the time of a negligent act. Henry Ford Hospital is not entitled to immunity for ordinary negligence because a hospital-patient relationship existed between the hospital and Dr. Hamburger at the time of the allegedly negligent acts of the hospital employees. The trial judge properly refused to give the defendant's requested instruction on gross negligence concerning the actions of the employees. Ordinary negligence, not gross negligence, was sufficient to establish hospital liability.

Our next illustration of the need for a safe working environment is based on the case of Mr. M.D., an 80-year-old male, who was transferred to a home for the aged in December, 1990. On admission, he wore a hearing aid, was confused at times, was ambulatory but had some orientation difficulties. He was characterized as having some dementia, was under several medications, and it was noted that he had an organic brain syndrome and was very shy.

One December, 1990 morning at 5:00 a.m., it was discovered that he had fallen while going to the bathroom, which was down the hall from his room. He was transferred to a local hospital, where they discovered he had a left shoulder fracture, a left hip fracture and a fractured pelvis. He was discharge from the local hospital at the end of January and went back to the nursing home in a stable condition.

A nurse's aide, in her deposition, pointed out that the patient was on the first floor, and that she was taking care of him as well as at least twenty other patients. He had no restraints, no bed rail, no nurses' call. There were also no night lights, no bars on the bed, and he had no cane, no walker, and no help in walking whatsoever. He had only been a resident for eight days prior to the incident and may not have even been sure of the way to the bathroom. We don't even know how long Mr. D. was on the floor before he was discovered by the nurse's aide at 5:00 a.m.

It was felt that the standard of care called for taking all necessary precautions in regard to the safety of the patient and following the regulations of the Michigan Department of Public Health on patient safety. It was also felt that there should have been careful analysis whether the patient belonged in this home, considering his inability to be alone most of the time with little attention by nurses or other staff.

Departures from the Standard of Care

We know that Mr. D. was confused, had problems with dementia, other previous psychiatric problems, and needed more attention than the average patient. We know also that this type of patient needs safety precautions much more than the average patient.

Mr. D. did not get adequate safety precautions - no bed rails, no nurses' call, no escort to the bathroom, no walker, no cane, no urinals, no restraints - in short, safety precautions were definitely insufficient.

Considering Mr. D.'s condition, two nurses' aides taking care of 47 patients was definitely insufficient, and he required a nursing home where he could get more care.

Insufficient actions were taken by this home. In short, there were serious departures from the standards of care for patients like Mr. D. It was felt that the failure to conform to good and acceptable practices as certainly a contributing cause to the fall of Mr. D., and the subsequent need for surgery and an extensive convalescent period.

More than likely, prevention could have allowed this patient to be discharged much earlier than January, 1991, and have eliminated the need for further rehabilitation, as well as the great inconvenience of having major surgery.

In conclusion, we have discussed various special problems - escapes from a long term care unit, the need for constant confidentiality in all health care settings, product liability and the problems caused by this, the statute of limitations as it applies to health care facilities, and finally, the need for safe working and patient environments at all times.

CHAPTER IX

NURSING HOMES

In the Fall of 1988, an interesting study was made of nursing homes provided by the American Health Care Association, in which members of corporate chains and hospital-affiliated facilities were over-represented. The postcards, which were sent out to 5,000 places, asked respondents to check whether or not their facility currently had in place a formal risk management system designed to eliminate or reduce legal and, hence, financial risks. 605 responses were received (12 percent), with 229 (38 percent) answering in the affirmative, and 376 (62 percent) in the negative. The results of this study are outlined in an article in Hospital and Health Services Administration Journal in the winter of 1990.

The nursing homes with risk management systems were more likely to be part of a chain or a hospital corporation than under independent ownership. Specifically, 96 percent of nursing homes with risk management systems were part of a chain or hospital corporation, while only 55 percent of nursing homes without systems were so owned. Furthermore, nursing homes with risk management systems were more likely to be accredited by the Joint Commission on Accreditation of Health Care Organizations than nursing homes without systems (16 vs 4 percent).

For those nursing homes claiming to have a risk management system, it is a relatively recent innovation. Within this group, mean number of years for the risk management system was only 6.1, with the maximum for one facility of twenty years.

Even more interesting were the characteristics outlined by the nursing homes with risk management systems.

Specific components were the following:

Written incident reports	95 percent
Written staff policies and procedures	95 percent
In-service training	93 percent
Employee injury prevention programs	84 percent
Risk Management Committee	75 percent
Incident reports used for trend analysis	63 percent
Purchase liability insurance	62 percent
Purchase Directors and Officers liability insurance	47 percent
Generic occurrence screening	43 percent
Self-insured for liability	32 percent
Self-insured for Officers and Directors liability	29 percent
Institutional Ethics Committee	25 percent

The responsibility for the risk management program was centered in the administrator at 71 percent, in the parent corporation or hospital at 37 percent, in a quality assurance coordinator for 30 percent, and in a risk manager for 16 percent. Legal counsel was integrated in risk management in 37 percent of the institutions.

When queried whether they believe that their risk management system had helped to improve the quality of care, 86 percent (65 of the 76) of the facilities in this category answered in the affirmative. 90 percent (68 of the 76) of the respondents opined that the existence of a risk management system improved their ability to administer the facility. 58 percent (44 of the 76) of the administrators felt that their risk management program helped to prevent or reduce the severity of lawsuits against the facility.

Most notably, 90 percent (68 of the 76) of the administrators answered that development of a formal risk management system within their facility had been worth the expense and effort involved and that they would recommend a risk management system to their colleagues.

Members of the "no-risk management" group were asked for reasons why they had not (at least knowingly) yet instituted a risk-management system. The following explanations were given: Fear of excessive implementation costs (22 percent), insufficient reimbursement (19 percent), concern about the threat of lawsuits was not serious enough to inspire a risk-management system (24 percent), and one-third (53 of the 160) of responding nursing homes without a formal risk-management system had never considered the subject, and 47 of the 124 respondents indicated that they planned to implement a risk-management system within the next three years.

In general, we are finding that lawsuits or malpractice issues against nursing homes are relatively new, but they are growing and are becoming more serious as nursing homes tend to become part of chains or are hospital organized.

Moreover, we are finding that federal juries in various states are awarding damage verdicts to families of nursing home patients who were neglected at a home run by some of the large chains. Some of the deaths caused by gross negligence are suddenly being used by attorneys to seek damages from the nursing homes. In an article in the *Detroit Free Press*, on July 12, 1990, Trish Nemore of the National Senior Citizens Law Center, an advocacy group in Washington, stated that damages were awarded in Mississippi for what happens to residents in maybe 60 percent of the nation's nursing homes. This case that was awarded against the nursing home in Mississippi was held to be a very important case because it didn't involve spectacular outrages, but the much more commonplace older people are subjected to as part of daily life in a nursing home, like not having call bells answered or not getting cleaned up after an accident. A case was made on the poor quality of life in the nursing home. Cases cited involved Beverly Enterprises, which operates over 800 nursing homes nationwide.

There have been a new series of lawsuits because of medication errors. It has been pointed out that complications caused by medication errors cost millions of dollars per year, and although a fatal medication occurs in only one out of 15 million drug doses, a recent study conducted in New York State, reported that medication errors resulted in 26 deaths in that state in 1989.

It is felt that a lot more medication errors result because of drug name mixups, as there are so many drugs available. Other common causes are breakdowns in oral and written communications and misidentifications in patients.

Such errors occur in nursing homes as well as in hospitals and other health care institutions.

One of the authors cited a series of cases that involved nursing homes. One of those was a patient named A.B., who was at a Veterans Administration nursing home and left the nursing home following a bingo game, and then was found frozen to death the next morning. The nursing home, which belonged to the federal government, was sued and a maximum claim was won.

This case could have been avoided if the institution had followed certain precautions. Specifically, they could have secured doors so that an alarm went off if anyone left. This would have been heard at the nursing station and an investigation would have followed immediately. Moreover, the institution should have been required to check patients in bed at certain hours. If the patient was missing at 9:30 p.m., an hour after he should have been in bed, an investigation should have found him long before the next morning.

The patient was known to have been confused as to time and place, was disoriented, and therefore possibly should have had a posey belt or a bedside rail, or special observation so that when he was missing a few hours after he went to a bingo game, he could have easily been located shortly afterwards. Perhaps he should have been chairfast or bedfast, as he was constantly wandering and was found in the wrong bed and on the wrong floors. As he had packed his belongings several times to leave, the institution should have taken steps to institute close observation so even if he did leave he would be found immediately afterward. The doctor in this case had written potentially the patient may physically injure himself, and yet nothing was done. The patient was allowed to go about in regular clothing, instead of any hospital or nursing home garb, and therefore really required some extra observation by a staff member, a volunteer, visitors, family or whatever. There is no question that the nursing home could have prevented this patient from leaving and by simply having him accompanied when he went out of the ward or returned from his bingo game, they would have avoided the problem.

Another nursing home case is mentioned in Chapter III. This involves a patient named W.W., who was an 81-year-old white female, who had suffered from a variety of illnesses during her lifetime. The most debilitating was a classic rheumatoid arthritis with total deformities since childhood. She lived with her family until she was admitted to a convalescent center in Wayne, Michigan, after suffering back injuries due to a fall at home. She recovered from these injuries, but fared well in the nursing home environment and remained there several years. At that time, she suffered a broken right fibula during an episode with another patient, and was transferred to Annapolis Hospital and then to a continued care center in Wayne, Michigan. In September 1986, the patient was being moved in a wheelchair by an aide, when she struck the area of her right knee on the wall and suffered a fracture at the neck of the fibula. When the family was contacted, Mrs. W. told her nephew that she thought the aide was angry at her for making too many requests, that she was being pushed too fast down the hallway, and that she was pushed into the wall. She heard a crack from her right knee and felt immediate pain. This version of the facts is substantiated by the nursing home's own records, in an incident report and somewhat by the nursing notes, and also by the emergency room report at the local hospital, where she was transferred. The aide indicated that Mrs. W. stuck out her leg to stop the wheelchair and had caused her own injury.

From the hospital, Mrs. W. was transferred to another nursing home and tended to deteriorate markedly, both mentally and physically. She was virtually bedridden, with some time spent in a wheelchair and could not wash herself. She used a bedpan, she was not fluently conversant, as she had been, she had trouble recognizing family, and constantly mumbled a chant which sounded like "Oh, Maria!" Her family described her as having lost her spirit to remain mentally and physically active and she was deteriorating rapidly in all respects.

We feel that this patient could have avoided her deterioration had she been taken care of properly in the nursing home. Certainly the aide, for whatever reason, should not have been rushing rapidly with the patient in a wheelchair.

The failure to conform to good and accepted nursing home practice was the probable cause of the many changes that occurred to Mrs. W.

Without a doubt, a simple incident which occurred to Mrs. W.W. is duplicated in many nursing homes throughout the country. We are indeed fortunate that the families of such patients do not sue as readily as they would in a hospital situation.

Another nursing home case involved a relatively simple situation which led to a death. Specifically, a 64-year-old patient named Mrs. W. Smith was admitted in 1985 to a convalescent center in the heart of Detroit. She remained there for several years and was know to be a chronic smoker. While she was occasionally urged not to smoke in certain areas, proper and full controls were not instituted, so that many times she smoked unobserved, often stole cigarettes from the nursing station, was able to leave the home and secure cigarettes from a neighboring store. There were notes in the chart that she should be watched carefully, but no efforts were made for her to stop smoking. On one occasion, she went to the back of the nursing home, walked out through the rear door, and started smoking outside. She apparently dropped a cigarette from her trembling hands onto her dress and it caught fire. She was transferred to a hospital and died a month later.

This patient should not have been exposed to the tragedy that occurred. Undoubtedly, she was not watched all the time. We are sure that incidents of patients smoking in unauthorized areas occur in many nursing homes, and are undoubtedly very difficult to control. Nonetheless, all nursing homes would be subject to lawsuits if such things did occur. Efforts must be made to reduce the incidents to an absolute minimum.

Our next case involves a patient who was in a home for the aged. This patient was a black male, aged 80. He was transferred in December 1990 to a home for the aged on the East side of Detroit. On his admission, he wore a hearing aid, was confused at times, was ambulatory but had some orientation difficulties. He was characterized as having some dementia, was under several medications, and it was noted that he had an organic brain syndrome and was very shy.

In December 1990, during the night, it was discovered that he had fallen while going to the bathroom, which was down the hall from his room. He was transferred to a local hospital, where they discovered that he had a left shoulder fracture, left hip fracture, and a fractured pelvis. He was discharged a month later, back to the home for the aged, in a stable condition.

The nurse's aide pointed out that the patient was on the first floor, and that she was taking care of him as well as twenty other residents. He had not been under any restraints, had no bedrail, had no nurses' call. There were also no night lights, no bars on the bed, and he had no cane, no walker, and no help in walking whatsoever. He had only been a resident eight days prior to the incident and may not have been sure of the way to the bathroom. We don't even know how long he had been on the floor before he was discovered by the nurse's aide at 5:00 a.m.

It was felt that not all necessary precautions in regard to the safety of the patient were followed in this case. There was a need for carefully analyzing whether the patient belonged in a home for the aged, considering his inability to be alone most of the time, with little attention by nurses or other staff. We know that he was confused, had problems with dementia, had other previous psychiatric problems, and needed more attention than the average patient. We know that this type of patient needs safety precautions much more than the average patient. His lack of bedrails, of nurse's call, no escort to the bathroom, no walker, no canes, no urinals, and no restraints, indicate that safety precautions were definitely insufficient.

Considering his condition, the two nurse's aides taking are of 47 patients in this home for the aged was definitely insufficient. He required a nursing home where he could get more care. We felt that insufficient actions to prevent falls were taken by this home. In short, there were serious departures from the standards of care for patients like Mr. D. He ended up having major surgery and a long period of rehabilitation. Yet, when we think of it, we are sure that this type of situation occurs in many nursing homes and in other homes for the aged. We are indeed fortunate that there are not many more lawsuits accordingly.

Let us cite another common situation. We have an 83-year-old woman who went to a nursing home after surgery to remove a brain tumor. After staying at the nursing home for approximately thirty days, she was discovered by the nursing staff to have a severe laceration of her eye. Ultimately she was forced to have the eye removed at a local hospital. There were no witnesses and the plaintiff was incompetent - unable to even explain what happened. The defendants now claim that the eye ruptured as a result of the accumulation of blood following surgery. An eye surgeon was consulted and he indicated that this was impossible. The expert witness in the case indicated that regardless of how the patient was injured - whether she did it to herself, was hurt by a fellow patient in the same room, was hurt by a visitor, or even by an employee - the nursing home was responsible, and undoubtedly will settle privately on this case or will lose the case in court.

It should be noted that despite the age of the patient, the settlement in this case was in the thousands of dollars.

Another case worth discussing is much more unusual. Mr. D.S. suffered from Alzheimer's disease, and as a result required nursing home care. He was a patient at a local nursing home in Detroit until June 1990, when he was found by a member of the staff to be unresponsive, sitting tethered to a chair in his room. An ambulance transported Mr. S. to Henry Ford Hospital, where he was pronounced dead. The E.R. physician discovered a rubber glove in Mr. S.'s trachea. An autopsy subsequently revealed that there were two more rubber gloves in his stomach.

Mr. S.'s medical records show that the nursing home staff was aware that he had an oral fixation and put things such as "paper plates, styrofoam cups, etc." in his mouth.

After Mr. S.'s death, the nursing home was cited by the State Health Department, and among other things, the nursing home implemented what they call a "PICA policy," concerning care plans for patients with known oral fixations.

This patient's death could have been avoided. The nursing home was very much puzzled that surgeons gloves were found in his body and could not explain how this could have occurred. Possibly a housekeeping aide or a nursing staff member left the gloves on a table near the patient. The patient was wheelchair-ridden and virtually bed-ridden, and could not possible have left the bed for any distance. In any case, the nursing home was considered negligent in allowing the patient to have access to such items.

The incident that occurred to Mr. D.S., in which he swallowed a foreign object which led to his death, could easily have occurred in many nursing homes. As expected, that as lawsuits become more prevalent in the nursing home field, incidents of this kind will lead to lawsuits.

Finally, we wish to detail a case of an 86-year-old who entered a nursing home from a hospital in December of 1990. Mrs. F. was relatively healthy until 1983, when she had a CVA. She recovered fairly well from this incident but had another CVA in August of 1990 and had to be hospitalized. She had decreased alertness and dehydration but was able to transfer to a nursing home in December 1990. She did have dementia and impaired speech following the CVA.

At the nursing home, Mrs. F was able to follow through with simple directions and at times appeared to comprehend what was said to her. Her speech was impaired due to the CVA but some limited verbalization was noted. She was wheelchair-bound but was receiving physical therapy five days a week, and attended occupational therapy five days a week for ambulatory training. She was noted to be improving in this regard and the occupational therapist encouraged patient involvement, tried to get her to dress and feed herself.. However, she was unresponsive a great deal of the time. She had to be fed and there were different degrees of awareness so that she was often noted to be confused, although it would appear to depend on the day. She often would kick the nurses and yell, although she was quiet when left alone. Her diet was changed a number of times but she tended to push away the staff and was uncooperative, especially in January 1991. She closed her mouth tightly and refused to eat. The nutritional department in December 1990 noted that she was confused, and that her alertness depended on the day and varied extensively. She vomited often with undigested food and was uncomfortable, but there was no rectal impaction and her abdomen showed no problems. The nursing home record indicates that Mrs. F. was discharged in January 1991, because of vomiting and abdominal pain. She was noted to be alert with some cognitive impairment. She was able to express her discomfort and she was informed that she needed hospitalization.

At a local hospital it was discovered that she had swallowed a three-inch-long chicken bone. To remove the bone Mrs. F. underwent two major surgeries. One involved an excision of a portion of the intestine in January 1991. In the second surgery, on February 15, she underwent the surgical creation of a passage (Anastomosis) between the stomach and the jejunum. She was then returned to another nursing home and died shortly afterwards.

Although it was clearly indicated in the chart that this patient was to be supervised at all meals and monitored, apparently this was not followed too carefully, and the patient swallowed a chicken bone that caused her great pain and suffering. Apparently since she was transferred to another nursing home on discharge from the hospital, it was felt by the family that she was not getting adequate care at the first nursing home. She should have been much more carefully followed, especially when eating. It is our feeling that there was a failure of good and acceptable nursing home practice, and this was a contributing cause to the pain and suffering endured by Mrs. F., and the need for hospitalization and special treatment in the hospital. More than likely, prevention could have allowed this patient to stay at the nursing home and eliminated the need for hospitalization, special surgery, as well as the great inconvenience and pain and suffering of having to be transferred to the hospital and subsequently to another nursing home.

Again, we find an incident which could have been easily repeated in many nursing homes.

The seven incidents described earlier, as well as the one incident in the home for the aged, illustrate situations which occur in other nursing homes and we believe will lead to more lawsuits in this field. This will be especially true as more chains are created, more hospitals establish their own nursing homes, and long-term insurance coverage becomes more prevalent.

CHAPTER X

DISCHARGE OF EMPLOYEES

It has been reported that 25% of all claims against hospital directors and officers involve wrongful termination of employees.[1] A basic cause of these suits is that employers are negligent in completing performance ratings in order to avoid paying severance, unemployment insurance and other perquisites.[2] Most wrongful discharge cases are based upon an employers breach of an express or implied employment contract.[3] An underlying concept in these cases is the principle known as the employment-at-will doctrine. This doctrine states that employment by an employer is indefinite, is for an unspecified duration and is entirely at the will of the employer or of the employee. Either the employer or the employee can terminate the employment relationship at any time without any reason, without notice or without cause.[4] However, as we shall see, there have been a number of court decisions interpreting this doctrine of which the health care administrator should be aware.

The basic case concerning this concept, Toussant v. Blue Cross and Blue Shield of Michigan, occurred in 1980. In this case "the

---

[1] AHA News, 27:1, February 25, 1991.

[2] Halliday, Jean. "Wrongful-discharge suits on the rise." Crain's Detroit Business, February 25, 1991, Page 3.

[3] Chard, Lynn and Etheridge, Barbara (eds). Wrongful Discharge Cases in Michigan, Ann Arbor, Institute of Continuing Legal Education, 1984, page 2.

[4] Ibid, page 3.

Michigan Supreme Court held that even in employment contracts of unspecified or indefinite duration an employee could enforce an employer's promise not to discharge except for just cause... Prior to Toussant, if an employee did not have a written employment agreement, the employment was presumed to be at will."[5]

As mentioned above, the courts have progressively limited the employment-at-will doctrine as increasing numbers of employees have challenged their terminations. Courts have recognized and applied several exceptions to the employer's right to terminate at-will employees. These exceptions include discharges that violate public policy, are motivated by an employer's bad faith or malice and those that breach an implied employment contract.[6] This chapter will review a number of those cases.

The courts have found that it is unlawful to dismiss an employee due to violation of public policy. In the case of Murray v. Bridgeport Hospital, which was decided in January, 1984, the Connecticut Supreme Court declared that in the case of a "plaintiff who was discharged from employment at the defendant Bridgeport Hospital the employment contract was for an indefinite duration and was terminable at will As a general rule, contracts of permanent employment, or for an indefinite term, are terminable at will, reflecting the view that an employer has the absolute right to run his business as he sees fit... In Sheets v. Teddy's Frosted Foods, Inc.... the court carved out an exception to the employment at will doctrine and held that an 'employer (may) be responsible in damages if the former employee can prove a demonstrably improper reason for dismissal, a reason whose impropriety is derived from some important violation of public policy.' Consequently, public policy imposes some limits on an employer's unfettered discretion to terminate the employment of someone hired at will."

An example of just what "public policy" is can be found in the following case of Wagenseller v. Scottsdale Memorial Hospital (Arizona, 1985):

---

5 Ibid, pages 3-4.

6 Heshizer, Brian. "The New Common Law of Employment: Changes in the Concept of Employment at Will." Labor Law Journal, 36:95, February, 1985.

"Catherine Wagenseller began her employment at Scottsdale Memorial Hospital as a staff nurse in March 1975, having been personally recruited by the manager of the emergency department, Kay Smith. Wagenseller was an "at-will" employee - one hired without specific contractual term. Smith was her supervisor. In August 1978, Wagenseller was assigned to the position of ambulance charge nurse, and approximately one year later was promoted to the position of paramedic coordinator... Three months later, on November 1, 1979, Wagenseller was terminated.

"Most of the events surrounding Wagenseller's work at the Hospital and her subsequent termination are not disputed, although the parties differ in their interpretation of the inferences to be drawn from and significance of these events. For more than four years, Smith and Wagenseller maintained a friendly, professional working relationship. In May 1979, they joined a group consisting largely of personnel from other hospitals for an eight-day camping and rafting trip down the Colorado River. According to Wagenseller, 'an uncomfortable feeling' developed between her and Smith as the trip progressed - a feeling that Wagenseller ascribed to 'the behavior that Kay Smith was displaying.' Wagenseller states that this included public urination, defecation and bathing, heavy drinking and 'grouping up' with other rafters. Wagenseller did not participate in any of these activities. She also refused to join in the group's staging of a parody of the song "Moon River,' which allegedly concluded with members of the group 'mooning' the audience...

"Wagenseller contends that her refusal to engage in these activities caused her relationship with Smith to deteriorate and was the proximate cause of her termination. She claims that following the river trip Smith began harassing her, using abusive language and embarrassing her in the company of other staff. Other emergency department staff reported a similar marked change in Smith's behavior toward Wagenseller after the trip, although Smith denied it.

"Up to the time of the river trip, Wagenseller had received consistently favorable job performance evaluations. Two months before the trip, Smith completed an annual evaluation report in which she rated Wagenseller's performance as 'exceeding results expected,' the second highest of five possible ratings. In August and October 1979, Wagenseller met first with Smith and then with Smith's successor, Jeannie Steindorff to discuss some problems regarding her duties... and her attitude toward the job. On November 1, 1979, following an exit interview at which Wagenseller was asked to resign and refused, she was terminated.

"She appealed her dismissal... claiming violations of the disciplinary procedure contained in the Hospital's personnel policy manual and requesting reinstatement and other remedies. When this appeal was denied, Wagenseller brought suit against the Hospital, its personnel administration, and her supervisor Kay Smith.

"Wagenseller, an "at-will" employee, contends that she was fired for reasons which contravene public policy and without legitimate cause related to job performance... The Hospital argues that an 'at-will' employee may be fired for cause, without cause, or for 'bad' cause. We hold that in the absence of contractual provision such an employee may be fired for good cause or for no cause, but not for 'bad' cause.

"The trend has been to modify the at-will rule by creating exceptions to its operation. Three general exceptions have developed. The most widely accepted approach is the 'public policy' exception, which permits recovery upon a finding that the employer's conduct undermined some important public policy. The second exception... requires proof of an implied-in-fact promise of employment for a specific duration... including assurances of job security in company personnel manuals or memoranda. Under the third approach, courts have found in the employment contract an implied-in-law covenant of 'good faith and fair dealing' and have held employers liable in both contract and tort for breach of that covenant. Wagenseller raises all three doctrines.

"...In the case before us, Wagenseller refused to participate in activities which arguable would have violated our indecent exposure statute... She claims that she was fired because of this refusal... The statute does... recognize bodily privacy as a 'citizen's social right.' ...We thus uphold this state's public by holding that termination for refusal to commit an act which might violate (the statute) may provide the basis of a claim for wrongful discharge. The relevant inquiry here is not whether the alleged 'mooning' incidents were either felonies or misdemeanors or constituted purely technical violations of the statute, but whether they contravened the important public policy interests embodied in the law."

The employment handbook which many health care facilities give to their employees generally outlines the rules and regulations of the institution, as well as the benefits an employee can enjoy (i.e. vacation, sick leave, holidays, insurance, etc.) The handbook, it has been decided by the courts, is a legal contract between the employer and the employee. This is clearly outlined in the court's decision in Fletcher v Wesley Medical Center, a case decided in the U.S. District Court in Kansas in May 1984:

> "Plaintiff Yvonne Fletcher claims... that she was discharged by defendant Becky Loosen from her employment as a secretary for defendant Wesley Medical Center, Inc., in violation of the Age Discrimination in Employment Act 29 U.S.C. 621... and for breach of express and implied covenants of job security.
>
> "...Plaintiff's... claim, grounded in a theory of contract implied in fact, is that statements in the Wesley Medical Center Employee Handbook limit the reasons for which employees can be fired, guarantee them elaborate grievance procedures to contest any proposed terminations, and promise two weeks' notice of any termination (except in cases of extreme employee misconduct). Unfortunately, the record before the Court as to exactly how defendants are supposed to have breached these ostensible promises is murky... moreover, the entire employee handbook has not been placed before the court by either party. Defendants appear to concede, however,... that they have not fully complied with the handbook's provisions; they argue, rather, that no matter what the manual says as regards job security, not one word of it is binding on them... (T)he Kansas Supreme Court has... indicated... in a case involving post-termination compensation:
>
> Ms. Sweet was provided with a copy of Stormont-Vail's employee handbook which set forth the general terms and conditions of employment. No one seriously questions the applicability of the employee hand-book to Ms. Sweet's employment. In fact, both parties rely upon the provisions of the handbook to support their positions and the provisions of the handbook may clearly be considered a part of the employment contract between Ms. Sweet and Stormont-Vail.
>
> "...(1) the employment relationship is terminable at the will of either party, absent a contract to the contrary... (2) employer statements that 'this is not seasonal employment' do not imply a

promise of lifetime employment... and (3) an employer has just cause to dismiss an employee who has refused to obey his supervisor's orders, where such conduct is expressly specified as grounds for dismissal in the employer's company policy manual.'

"...The Court does not want to be misunderstood: it may well turn out that when the record is complete and the handbook provisions on which plaintiff relies are put in proper factual context, the absence of any contractual agreement regarding job security will be evident. For example, appropriate express disclaimers could make it obvious that the employer was not giving up its right to fire at will... or the ostensible promises made by the employer might be so vague and meaningless as to be unenforceable."

An interesting wrongful discharge case which had not been published at the time this manuscript was prepared is Brandt v. North Detroit General Hospital (Michigan, 1991). In this case the discharge took place as part of a general reduction in the hospital's workforce due to a poor census. However, because the hospital had simultaneously granted large salary increases to top management the hospital lost the case as well as having $200,000 awarded to the plaintiff employee.[7]

Another case of discharge due to a hospital reducing its staff because of economic constraints is Bhogaonker v. Metropolitan Hospital (Michigan, 1988):

"The case arises out of the termination of plaintiff's employment as a physician by defendant, Metropolitan Hospital. Plaintiff is a medical doctor licensed to practice in the State of Michigan. In November, 1974, when plaintiff was hired by defendant as a physician, defendant indicated that it would provide him with employment so long as his work was satisfactory. Plaintiff successfully completed the two-year probationary period specified in the medical staff by-laws of defendant hospital. He thereupon received a permanent appointment as of November, 1976, subject to termination only for good cause.

[7] Nursing Home Update. Health Care Association of Michigan. 16:4, July 5, 1991.

"In 1981, plaintiff's employment was terminated by defendant because of a reduction in staff due to budget cuts. The 1981-82 expense budget of the hospital had to be reduced by $4,000,000. There was no factual dispute that plaintiff's employment was terminated because of economic reasons which resulted in staff reduction.

"On May 9, 1984, plaintiff filed a complaint against defendant alleging that defendant terminated plaintiff's employment without cause and thus violated its contractual obligations. Plaintiff alleged five counts: breach of contract, estoppel, breach of covenant of good faith and fair dealing, negligence, and, alternatively, that defendant failed to give adequate notice of the termination and failed to pay all benefits due and owing to plaintiff upon termination.

"...(1) We first note that... there was no dispute as to any material facts and defendant was entitled to judgment as a matter of law. Plaintiff did not and does not contest the economic necessity for the termination of his employment... Case law indicates that termination of the employment of an otherwise competent employee due to an economically motivated business closing is not grounds for a wrongful discharge claim... We find that... as a matter of law, plaintiff's discharge for economic reasons, as determined by and within the complete discretion of the board of directors of defendant corporation constitutes termination for sufficient cause. To hold otherwise would impose an unworkable economic burden upon employers to stay in business to the point of bankruptcy in order to satisfy employment contracts and related agreements terminable only for good or sufficient cause."

In another case, McQuarry v. BelAir Convalescent Home, the Oregon Court of Appeals in July 1984 decided a case in an employees favor who had been discharged for what is commonly known as "whistleblowing." The court, in this case, indicated:

"Defendant is a licensed intermediate care nursing home. Plaintiff was employed as defendant's In-Service Director of Nurses Training and Education. In December, 1979, plaintiff's aunt became a patient at the care center. In the same month, Samuel Lissitz became the home's administrator. Early in the morning of January 26, 1980, a fire broke out in a wastebasket in a corridor near the room Plaintiff's aunt occupied. Lissitz concluded that plaintiff's aunt had started the fire by careless smoking and ordered her transferred from the home. Plaintiff was off duty but came to the home when she learned of the transfer. Due to her intercession, her aunt was returned to the home; after a heated conversation with Lissitz, plaintiff agreed to stay at the home that evening until her aunt went to sleep.

"The next day... the facility's fire sprinkler system broke down because of frozen pipes, and the fire department ordered a 24 hour fire watch until it was operable. Plaintiff was again off duty. Plaintiff's aunt called her at her home to complain that Lissitz was yelling at the aunt and calling her a fire bug. Plaintiff came to the care center. After another heated conversation, in the course of which plaintiff threatened to report his actions toward her aunt to the Health Division. Lissitz fired her. His action is the basis for her claim.

"...The first issue is whether a discharge for such a threat is actionable. An employer may not discharge an employee for fulfilling a societal obligation... The evidence in this case would permit a jury to find that Lissitz discharged plaintiff because she had threatened to report his actions to the Health Division and that she believed in good faith that his actions violated her aunt's rights under the Nursing Home Patient's Bill of Rights... The Health Division is charged with protecting patients' rights under the act... and a report to it would be societal obligation of a person who knows of violations... (P)rotection is an important public policy analogous to the performance of jury duty or the avoidance of defamation, policies which the Supreme Court has found to justify wrongful discharge claims... A discharge for reporting a violation of that policy to the proper authority would thus be a discharge for fulfilling a societal obligation and would be actionable.

"(W)e believe that the social harm from reporting in good faith a complaint that may turn out, after investigation, to be unfounded is potentially far less than the harm of not reporting a well-founded complaint for fear of the consequences. The social benefit from investigating all potentially significant violations of a patient's statutory rights is far greater than the social benefit, if any, from allowing an employer to terminate an employee who in good faith reports to the appropriate authorities situations which prove not to be violations. We therefore hold that an employee is

> protected from discharge for good faith reporting of what the employee believes to be patient mistreatment to an appropriate authority."

Many times probationary employees are dismissed without notice and without cause. Although, this is a common practice caution must still be used by the employer to avoid vindictiveness and to investigate each case completely prior to taking final action. This is well illustrated in the case of Crenshaw v. Bozeman Deaconess Hospital (December, 1984):

> "On December 1, 1981, Crenshaw commenced employment with the Hospital as a respiratory therapist. Prior to that time, she had been employed by an independently operated respiratory therapy department which contracted services to the hospital. The department was purchased by the Hospital on December 1, 1981. Crenshaw worked for the Hospital until January 8, 1982, at which time she took a leave of absence until February 8, 1982. After returning to work, Crenshaw was employed until March 12, 1982, when she was discharged.
>
> "Subsequent to the take-over of the respiratory department by the Hospital two orientation meetings were held with employees of the respiratory department... The employees were given a personnel manual. A provision in the manual provided: 'You are on probation during the first 500 hours of employment. Any employee may be discharged without notice during the probationary period.' Both parties concur that Crenshaw had not completed the 500 hours of probationary status at the time of her discharge...
>
> "The immediate dispute began in the late hours of March 11, 1982. Three nurses on duty in the intensive care unit complained to their supervisor... A meeting was held between... (the supervisor), the three nurses, ... the personnel director and... the acting head of the respiratory therapy department. Following the meeting, a discharge memorandum was prepared directing Crenshaw's discharge. The discharge document charged Crenshaw with: 'Insubordination; disrupting the continuity of care; continually getting in the way of patient care; disorderly conduct; unsatisfactory work performance; violation of safety and/or health rules; and breach of confidentially.'

"The testimony reveals, on the night of March 11, 1982, Crenshaw was not at home when the Hospital attempted to reach her at 10:30 p.m. That evening Crenshaw had been visiting a former patient. Crenshaw's husband telephoned her to tell her that the Hospital had called. Crenshaw telephoned the Hospital and was told that she would be needed at the Hospital later that evening, Crenshaw immediately departed for the hospital. The former patient's daughter, Berna-Dean Hennessey, drove her to the hospital. Hennessey remained at the Hospital for a number of hours. Related to Hennessey's presence, the discharge document charged Crenshaw with 'breach of confidentiality.' The Hospital contends a breach of confidential information resulted when Hennessey accompanied Crenshaw to the Hospital lab. While Crenshaw ran a separate errand, Hennessey waited for a blood-gas report and delivered it to the ICU. Crenshaw contends the report was not readily comprehensible to a lay person. Hennessey testified:

"(a) she did not examine the contents of the slip, (b) that upon arriving at the intensive care unit she put her hand inside the curtain and handed the slip to someone tending to patient care, and (c) that she did not at any time view the patient.'

"The 'insubordination' charge stemmed from the nurses' allegation that Crenshaw attempted to perform ABG's (arterial blood gases). This fact is disputed not only by Crenshaw, but by the nurses and doctors present...

"The discharge document also accused Crenshaw of not performing 'the respiratory therapy task of suction as needed.' Again there was a dispute as to whether suctioning was called for. The nurses testified that the suctioning should have been performed for the sake of appearance of the patient. However, one of the physicians testified that suctioning was not required...

"The three nurses present during the shift, also charged that Crenshaw was disrupting the continuity of patient care. As a result, Crenshaw was accused of 'endangering patient well-being.' The nurses testified that Crenshaw repeatedly answered the telephone, read electrocardiogram monitors and distracted the nurses by commenting on the irregular cardiac display on the monitors. The testimony regarding this allegation is in conflict. Two physicians present during the controversial shift testified that they found nothing deficient about Crenshaw's performance. Also, one of the nurses in attendance during part of the shift, confirmed that there was no misbehavior on Crenshaw's part. Finally, the discharge document states that Crenshaw had been subject to previous verbal counselings. It was established at the trial, however, that this was false and that Crenshaw had not been subject to previous disciplinary action by the Hospital.

"The following morning, Crenshaw was called into the Hospital. Crenshaw was given the disciplinary discharge document and was advised to see the administrator the following Monday. On Monday, March 15, 1981, Crenshaw met with the administrator... He informed her that he would review the matter, the administrator conducted interviews of those present in the intensive care unit during the morning in question. The administrator affirmed the discharge in a letter to... Crenshaw... Crenshaw contends that the administrator failed to interview all of the staff members, even though he was aware that they had been present during the controversial shift and that the charges were strongly contested.

"After her discharge, Crenshaw applied for unemployment compensation benefits. Crenshaw alleges the Hospital informed the Bozeman Job Service indicating that she had been discharged for unsatisfactory performance and for endangering patient well-being. As a result, Crenshaw was unable to procure employment in the medical community in Bozeman. She encountered difficulties because of a lack of references from her previous employer. In January, 1983, she and her husband were forced to close his construction business and move to Spokane...

"Crenshaw contends the Hospital acted with malice; (1) by lodging and sustaining false charges against her; and (2) by tampering with her personnel file. Crenshaw claims a certificate authorizing her to perform arterial blood gases was removed from the file...

Crenshaw alleged the Hospital breached the implied covenant of good faith and fair dealing. She further alleged the actions of... (the Hospital) were negligent and were malicious and/or in wanton and/or in willful disregard of her rights entitling her to exemplary damages... A jury trial was held on November 28, 1983. The jury found for Crenshaw and awarded her $125,000 in compensatory damages and exemplary damages in the amount of $25,000."

The case was appealed by the Hospital to the Montana Supreme Court which rendered a decision for Crenshaw on December 6, 1984. (The above quotes are from that decision.) In upholding the decision of the jury the Supreme Court indicated the following:

> "(W)e hold even in probationary employment relationships, the employer still owes his employee a duty of good faith and fair dealing...
>
> "Employers can still terminate untenured employees at-will and without notice. They simply may not do so in bad faith or unfairly without becoming liable for damages. The Hospital's notification to the Bozeman Job Service of Crenshaw's unsatisfactory work performance deprived her of employment in the local medical community. This was an act of bad faith. The charges and allegations in the discharge memorandum were false. The charges were serious and resulted in Crenshaw losing her employment as well as jeopardizing her career. This was an act of bad faith. The record shows that Crenshaw's discharge was motivated by bad faith and warrants recovery for breach of implied covenant of good faith and fair dealing...
>
> "Crenshaw responds (that) the Hospital's failure to interview all of the witnesses present on the night in question was negligent as a theory separate and distinct from the theory of breach of good faith and fair dealing. Crenshaw offered evidence which raised the question of the Hospital's negligence:
>
> "(1) the former acting director testified he had not interviewed all of the appropriate witnesses;
>
> "(2) the administrator admitted that he had failed to interview key witnesses and that he was not sure he had interviewed a physician sustaining the discharge; and
>
> "(3)... Crenshaw's expert on personnel management conceded that 'when the discharge was made... the allegation had not been properly investigated by the hospital administrator.'
>
> "In light of the foregoing, we find the Hospital's conduct showed a 'want of attention to the nature or probable consequence of the act or omission' and that their conduct fell below the 'standard established by law for the protection of others against unreasonable risk."... The allegation of negligence was clearly established in respondent's complaint."

It can be seen from the above cases that an at will clause in a personnel policy handbook may not be enough to bring about a dismissal in court of a wrongful discharge claim by an employee. Most healthcare employers have instituted a progressive disciplinary process, which in current times is considered a fair and just procedure. However, if such a policy does exist then it must be followed and an employee can not be terminated without being given the privilege of using the policy. Even if an at will statement is given to the employee the disciplinary process, if also present, becomes precedent over the at will policy.

It is important to note that "these cases have become a large burden on the courts ever since the Toussaint decision, and the court is now trying to limit the right of employees to sue. However, it should be made clear at the outset of employment that the employee is an at will employee. This should be done in the application for employment that is signed by the employee, as well as any handbooks that are handed out."[8]

Advice to administrators can best be summed up by the following comments of Gary Miller[9]:

> "Employer-employee literature including job application forms, handbooks, personnel manuals, and benefits literature should establish within the first few pages, through so-called 'disclaimer' clauses, that the employer-employee relationship is 'at-will' with no promise of employment for any specific term. In addition, it should be clearly stipulated that any employment literature is not to be considered a contract.
>
> "To avoid potential 'implied contract' allegations, eliminate any 'discharge only for just cause' provisions or the equivalent from all employment related literature.
>
> "...Management at all levels of the patient care organization should be clearly informed not to make any statements guaranteeing employment or conditions such as 'termination only for just cause.'

---

[8] Nursing Home Update. Healthcare Association of Michigan, Lansing. November 1, 1991, page 2.

[9] Miller, Gary. "At-will Employment Doctrine-Are Patient Care Employers Vulnerable? Hospital & Health Services Administration. 36:268-69, Summer 1991.

> "...To best avoid... possible suits, managers should be aware of and respect employees' rights and duties, particularly those granted or required by statute. As the cases show, the most prominent examples of such rights and duties include the following: the right to file worker's compensation claims, the duty to answer subpoenas and summons, the duty (characterized as a right in some states) to report significant violations of laws or fraudulent conduct, and the duty to answer fully and honestly under oath. Discharges of employees for exercising or fulfilling these rights and duties are universally held to be wrongful."

A final, but exceedingly important caveat is to make absolutely sure that all discussions held with an employee concerning their work be documented. If any disciplinary action has been taken it too must be thoroughly documented and be a part of the employees personnel file. Without such documentation the employer has no evidence of past performance and action taken if the employee decides to take legal action concerning discharge.

Chapter XI

Nursing

John Griffith, in his Well-Managed Community Hospital, (1987) pointed out that the better the nursing, the sooner the patient will recover[1]. Nursing can make a substantial contribution to both quality and economy of care by prevention, supportive care, case management for outpatients, and by reduced use of other clinic-support services education and reassurance for patient and family, shorter stay, and discharge planning for inpatients.[2]

The great importance to patient care by nursing is stressed in several chapters. It is pointed out that nursing can maximize its contribution to patient care by taking the following steps:[3]

"-Establish measurement systems to provide routine guidance in patient care for each floor or unit. Particular attention should be paid to such clinical measures as:

- procedural quality measures, emphasizing the establishment and implementation of a patient care plan.
- patient satisfaction measures, assessing the acceptability of care, both for nursing and the hospital as a whole.

---

[1] Griffith, Well-Managed Community Hospital, p. 568.

[2] Ibid.

[3] Ibid p. 369-370.

- outcomes measures, reflecting both clinical and economic consequences, such as length of stay, cost per case, and re-admission.

    - Determine acceptable long term goals for these measures. Goals will depend upon exchange needs or community demand, as well as technical capabilities. Areas of greater deficiency will become priority concerns for annual improvement.
    - Negotiate practical improvements and expectations for priority concerns with head nurses in annual budget activities.
    - Study nursing activities and systems to identify ways in which further improvements can be made toward acceptable levels of performance. Opportunities include:

        - revising nursing procedures, equipment, and staffing.
        - improving personnel training and in-service education.
        - improving nursing care plans.
        - improving patient care information systems.
        - eliminating variability in patient care and treatment procedures.
        - increasing reassurance and encouragement to patients.
        - provide more extensive patient education.

    - Study other clinical service costs to find less costly ways of meeting acceptable performance levels. Better nursing can reduce laboratory work, drug usage, social service, respiratory therapy, and rehabilitation therapy requirements."

There have been a series of malpractice cases involving improper general care by the nursing department, and also a series of slips and falls which occurred to patients, possibly because nurses have not done their share of proper patient care.

We can best illustrate these concepts by a series of actual cases which occurred in the past few years. Please note that some of the above mentioned standards were not followed.

First is the case of Mr. S.S., a 68 year old married white male, admitted to the hospital in Lexington, Kentucky in July, 1985, for further chemotherapy for his known acute leukemia which was in relapse. He had initially been seen and diagnosed in May 1984 for his leukemia, which had entered into a complete remission following an induction course of medications. He was treated with concurrent low dosage heparin throughout his induction.

Before his admission in July, he had evidence of relapse, with a marked elevation in his white count, comprised entirely of promylelocytes and myeloblasts. He was again treated and showed some improvement which was noted to have occurred approximately ten days before he was readmitted. At the time of his second admission, he was admitted for further treatment of his relapsed acute leukemia. He also had a history of myocardial infarction.

After his admission to the hospital, it was noted that he had begun having substernal chest pains unrelieved with nitrogen and was therefore transferred to the coronary care unit. He showed some improvement under the care of his heart specialist and then was transferred back to a general medical floor. He remained there, and in August, after having his catheter flushed by a nurse, he subsequently developed cardiac arrest with ventricular fibrillation. He remained comatose, and later that evening, in August of 1985, he was pronounced dead.

On August 14th, his treating physician, Dr. C., was informed that the nurse who had flushed the Hickman catheter just before the episode of ventricular fibrillation advised her nursing supervisor earlier that day that she had by accident administered a potassium chloride solution instead of a hepranized saline solution four days earlier.

An investigation was conducted and the nurse who had injected the potassium chloride was terminated as a result of the medication error.

Standard of Care

In July and August of 1985, good and accepted hospital practice in the field of coronary care and internal medicine required that the hospital authorities in Lexington, Kentucky do certain things:

1. Maintain adequate controls on all medications, listing them, counting them, labeling them for each particular patient so that they can not possibly be used improperly or any substitution made. A further control has be to instituted when a patient is transferred from one unit to another. When a patient is transferred from a CCU unit to a general medical floor, the particular medicine must be counted, labeled, and identified in such a way that no possible error can be made when the patient arrives at his or her new unit.

2. Controls must be instituted in working with employees so that supervisors recognize when employees are not adequately functioning in their work. This may be due to physical or mental problems away from the hospital which interfere with their work. When employees are so tired that they begin to make mistakes, ways must be found to relieve them, at least temporarily, of their work so that they can recuperate and function adequately. It is the duty of every supervisor to watch each employee under their jurisdiction to determine that the person is functioning adequately.

3. Procedures should be established in the hospital to control the patient's relatives from spending the entire night sleeping in a patient's room, even if the patient is in serious or critical condition. Visitors who want to be in the hospital throughout the night should be separated and placed in a lounge where they can get rest and still be able to visit the patient on a periodic basis. Nurses must be able to perform their duties on patients, away from relatives when it is so indicated.

DEPARTURES FROM THE STANDARD OF CARE

The hospital personnel in this hospital in Lexington, Kentucky departed from good and accepted hospital practice in the following way:

1. They failed to properly institute controls on the transfer of medications from the CCU unit to the general medical floor. This meant that a number of medications followed Mr. S.S. to his medical unit floor which should not have been transferred there. The patient required certain medications in his new unit, but did not require potassium chloride, and this should have remained in the CCU unit. There should not have been any potassium chloride in the general medical unit. The failure of the hospital to prevent the transfer of the potassium chloride meant that it was available to the nurse and may have possibly been given erroneously to the patient.

2. The hospital should have recognized the fatigue of the nurse and stopped her from working overtime. It is noteworthy that they asked her to drop her private duty nursing, but did not ask her to stop her overtime. Granted that there may have been a need for her services, as there was an apparent shortage of nursing staff, it is likewise true that her continued work was a detriment to the hospital and to patients. When she asked for vacation relief, this was denied to her because apparently she did not have enough seniority, but a special consideration should have been made in view of her recognized tiredness by both the supervisor and fellow employees. The deposition of the nurse and her supervisor as shown in a hearing before the State Board of Nursing Personnel indicated that there were many discussions of her fatigue and the need for her getting help, but the hospital failed to act and her overtiredness may have contributed to her actions in regard to Mr. S.S.

3. Relatives should not have been permitted to stay in the same room as a seriously ill patient throughout the night, sleeping in the room, and possibly interfering with his care. Such relatives should have been permitted to visit on a regular basis, but not have remained in the same room.

4. Under the legal doctrine of Respondeat Superior (See Chapter II), the employer is responsible for the action of his employee. In this instance the hospital must be considered responsible for the actions of the nurse.

CAUSATIONS

The failure to conform to good and accepted hospital practice was the probable cause of the injury to and the death of Mr. S.S. Undoubtedly the error in medications hastened his death.

The patient, S.S., was transferred from the intensive care unit to a regular room in the hospital. The family was called in and was asked to help out in the transfer. Among other things, they were given a bag of medications. This was definitely improper. The medications should have been sent directly to the pharmacy or to the nursing station and not placed at the bedside table next to the patient. The patient was in his regular room a full ten days, before the nurse reached for the potassium chloride instead of a sodium chloride mixture. Had proper procedure been followed, there is no question that the nurse would not have made this error.

This case went to a jury trial, the hospital was found liable, and a sizable award was given to the family of Mr. S.S.

The next case involves a joint responsibility of the attending physician and nursing staff.

A BRIEF SUMMARY OF THE FACTS

Mrs. C.T. was seen in the emergency room of a hospital in Connecticut in March of 1984, by the emergency room physician. At that time she was approximately 26 weeks pregnant and after various tests were done, she was discharged to remain at strict bedrest and was asked to see her regular obstetrician the following day. She did return to the hospital the following day and was admitted in the evening. Examination revealed that she was ready to deliver and her regular physician, as well as her pediatrician, was informed, and a nearby Neonatal Intensive Care Unit was likewise informed.

A male infant was delivered in a breech position at 7:33 p.m. on March 9, 1984. The delivery was reportedly atraumatic. Dr. S. was in attendance and the initial Apgar test showed a heart rate of approximately forty. The child was taken to the Newborn Unit, where he was placed under a warmer, oxygen ordered and momentary bagging accomplished. At the time, Dr. S. did not believe that the infant was viable and did not order resuscitation.

However, the Neonatal Transfer Team from the nearby hospital arrived at 7:42 p.m. and started resuscitation with bagging. The child was resuscitated and placed on a respirator and transferred to the Neonatal Intensive Care Unit.

Despite the intensive care administered the next day, the baby was having difficulty in breathing. At 6:20 a.m. on March 11, 1984, the infant expired following continuing deterioration.

Other noteworthy considerations include: The pediatrician had decided not to do resuscitation despite an Apgar of one. The anesthetist or anesthesiologist was called an hour before delivery, but neither an anesthetist nor an anesthesiologist appeared. There was no follow up by the nursing staff to see if those who were called were coming in. It is not clear whether the pediatrician or the obstetrician requested an anesthesiologist to be present.

STANDARDS OF CARE

In March of 1984, good and accepted hospital practice in the field of Neonatal care and Obstetrics required that the hospital authorities at this hospital in Connecticut do the following things:

1. Analyze all the aspects of the patient's condition and the possible condition of her offspring at the time of delivery, and determine if extra help is needed for resuscitation, special care of the infant and the mother.

2. Notify any special personnel that might be required in the care of mother and infant should there be special circumstances due to the early gestation of the baby.

3. Follow up any calls to personnel asked to come to the delivery room for help with child or baby.

4. Once the infant is delivered to continue optimal care for the infant to include resuscitation and stabilization until it could be transferred to an intensive care nursery.

DEPARTURES FROM THE STANDARD OF CARE

1. Although a team of assistants, including an anesthetist, was requested a full hour before delivery, according to the nursing notes no one from the anesthesia department was present. Considering the severity of the case and possible trauma to the child, an anesthetist or anesthesiologist should have been present, called by the nursing staff or the physician.

2. If no one responded to the call by the nursing staff or the physician, there should have been a follow up to determine if the anesthetist or a suitable substitute would respond.

3. From the records, it seems that the pediatrician should have resuscitated immediately on this borderline case, but his failure to do so is not primarily the responsibility of the hospital, as the doctor is not an employee. Resuscitation of the newborn was apparently not accomplished on a timely basis.

CAUSATIONS

The failure to conform to good and acceptable hospital practice was certainly a contributing cause to the subsequent death of the patient.

We understand that at least 60% of twenty-six week gestational-age babies do survive. It is difficult to know whether this child would have survived had there been immediate resuscitation in the first minutes of life. However, more than likely, had there been an anesthetist or anesthesiologist present, the chances are that the baby would have survived beyond 36 hours after birth.

In this case, the nursing staff should have reminded the physician of the need for an anesthetist or anesthesiologist.

This case was settled privately against the hospital and the physicians involved.

Many times improper nursing care results in accidents.

The patient may slip or be hurt in some unusual way. We have selected two cases to illustrate this. The first is a case of a 34-year-old female, Mrs. M.O., who was admitted to the emergency room of a Detroit, Michigan hospital in the fall of 1987, with complaints of lower abdominal pain and vaginal spotting. She had been seen a week earlier by a physician at his clinic located nearby, to diagnose her complaints of vaginal bleeding and nausea.

In September of 1987, the treating doctor in the emergency room performed a D & C in the emergency room on a regular hospital bed which did not have side railings to secure the plaintiff. At some point after the operation, Mrs. O., under the influence of anesthesia, fell off the hospital bed onto the floor, striking her head as well as other parts of her body. It seems that the nurse left the doctor in the room and said she was going out to get a stretcher, leaving the doctor alone with the patient. The doctor stepped outside the room to complete his chart, which was in a folder immediately outside the room. It was then that the patient fell off the table. It should be noted that there were no side rails, no belts to hold the patient, and no one else in the room. Certainly, the nurse could have easily pressed the nurse's call button and secured someone to either watch the patient or get the stretcher. She could have cautioned the doctor to keep an eye on the patient. In any case, the doctor was as responsible as the nurse, but an accident did occur and there is no question that it wasn't the patient's fault.

The patient was admitted to the hospital immediately thereafter in order to examine her for possible ectopic pregnancy. Surgery was performed by her doctor and the diagnosis after surgery was tubal pregnancy. A left salpingectomy was performed under a general anesthesia. Mrs. O. was discharged from the hospital in September, 1987. She was subsequently seen by a neurologist in October, 1987. At that time she complained of headaches, dizziness, memory difficulties, and nervousness. According to the neurological record, the headaches were bifrontal and vertex in location, throbbing in nature, and varied daily in duration from 2 to 24 hours. Other symptoms included blurred vision, especially of the right eye, nausea, lightheadness, nosebleeds and tension.

She was subsequently seen by Dr. P.T., a psychologist, to whom she was referred to by the neurologist.

Dr. T. saw the patient on July 1, July 8, July 15 and July 29, 1988. In her summary she writes:

> "In the patient's environment, minor disruptions will create major dysfunctioning. Due to significant impairment in higher level adaptive functioning abilities, she has difficulty adapting to new situations. When interrupted from a sequence of activity, she loses her pattern of thought, has significant difficulty adjusting to the newly presented situation, and does not readily pick back up with her original pattern of thought without cueing.
>
> "Difficulty is especially noted when she must sustain her attention to integrate information. In extremely demanding situations, these interference effects are profoundly disruptive. Because the patient is well aware of her weaknesses, stress (emotion and environmental) tends to worsen her difficulties.
>
> "The current pattern of results is suggestive of extremely high levels of anxiety. This pattern of difficulty is often typical of the performance of individuals who become hyper-reactive in response to significant stressors in a relatively short period of time. Decreased states of alertness, difficulty with emotional modulation, dizziness, and the resulting significant reduction in mental efficiency appear to be symptoms of extreme anxiety and depression that will impede environmental functions. The presence of mild organicity (brain trauma) cannot be ruled out. However, with the current high level of emotional dysfunction, it is difficult to determine the extent of possible organicity. "Diagnostic Impression: 309.61 Post Traumatic Stress Disorder, moderate Recommendations: 1. Therapeutic psychological intervention for the emotional distress currently evidenced is recommended. 2. Neuropsychological re-evaluation is recommended in 6 to 8 months

after psychological treatment to rule out the presence of postconcussional syndrome. 3. The patient should continue to be monitored by a neurologist for possible late occurring complications or post traumatic symptomatology (e.g., hydrocephalus, seizure activity). The optimum time period for risk is 6 to 18 months post traumatic incident. 4. Upon return to work, full-time responsibilities should be monitored for difficulties."

It should be noted that Mrs. O. had been serving adequately as a payroll clerk in hr job in Detroit until her injury in September 1987.

Standard of Care

In September 1987, good and accepted hospital practice in the field of medicine required that the hospital authorities of this hospital in Detroit, Michigan do certain things:

1. Establish adequate policies and procedures for emergency surgical patients to ensure proper treatment to avoid permanent injury.
2. Properly evaluate and train its staff nurses, anesthetist and any other employees and agents in the proper procedures for surgery performed under anesthesia.
3. Properly supervise employees and/or agents to ensure that the proper equipment is used.
4. Provide for the proper scrutiny, care, and treatment of patients, allowing them not to roll off beds while still under the effects of anesthesia.
5. Properly evaluate the qualifications of their physicians, not allowing any physician to perform surgery in a non-surgical setting.

Departures from the Standard of Care

The hospital personnel and physicians at this hospital in Detroit departed from good and accepted hospital practice in the following ways:

The hospital did provide emergency services but failed to have a staff adequately watch patients in the emergency area. It did not establish adequate policies and procedures so that these patients would secure proper treatment and not be injured in any way during the time that they were in the emergency area. The hospital failed to properly evaluate and train its staff nurses and other employees and agents in the way surgery should be performed under anesthesia and the way patients are taken care of in a surgical setting. This patient was not watched and was allowed to roll off the bed while still under the effects of anesthesia.

There were no side rails on the bed and it seems that this may simply have been a stretcher, not even a normal hospital bed, which is provided with side rails. Obviously a surgical bed should have been provided for patients who do have surgery in the emergency room. The patient was given an I.V. anesthesia and when she fell, she suffered facial and head trauma.

Even if a regular stretcher or simple hospital bed was used, someone should have been watching Mrs. O. after she had her D&C so that she could not possibly roll off the bed and hurt herself.

Under the legal doctrine of Respondeat Superior (See Chapter II), the employer is responsible for the actions of his employees. In this instance, the hospital must be considered responsible for the actions of the personnel in the emergency room and its agent, Dr. P.

Causations

The failure to conform to good and accepted hospital practice was the probable cause of the injury to Mrs. M.O. From all indications, she suffered severe head injuries and may have suffered some brain damage. From the observations of the psychologists almost a year after her injury, she apparently is still under the effect of her fall.

This case was privately settled, out of court, following the expert testimony of one of the authors of this book, in January, 1990. The defendant hospital paid!

We next have an interesting nursing home case, involving an incident similar to that which occurs in other nursing homes.

A Brief Summary of the Facts

Ms. W.W. is an 81-year-old female who was a patient at a continued care center in September, 1986. She previously lived with her family until she was admitted to a convalescent center after suffering back injuries due to a fall at home. She recovered from this injury and fared well in the nursing home environment, and remained at the convalescent center until September, 1984. At that time, she suffered a broken right fibula during an episode with another patient. She was transferred to a hospital, then to the continued care center.

In time she recovered admirably from her broken leg. While she did require assistance, she was eventually able to walk somewhat with a cane, to go to the dining room and bathroom and socialize. She was mentally alert.

On September 28, 1986, Ms. W. was being moved in a wheelchair by an aide when she struck the area of her right knee on a wall, and suffered a fracture at the neck of the fibula. Her family was contacted by the personnel and her nephew, B.G. arrived. Ms. W. told him that she thought the aide was angry at her for making too many requests; that she was being pushed too fast down the hallway in her wheelchair, and that she was pushed into the wall. She heard a crack from her right knee and felt immediate pain. This version of the facts is verified by the convalescent center's own records (Incident Report and by the Nursing Notes), and also by the Emergency Room Report at the hospital, where she was transferred. Later, the Aide stated that Ms. W. stuck out her leg to stop the wheelchair and caused her own injury.

From the hospital, Ms. W. was transferred to a nursing home in October, 1986. She has deteriorated markedly, both mentally and physically. She is virtually bedridden, with some time spent sitting in a wheelchair. She cannot wash herself. She uses a bedpan. She is not fluently conversant, as she had been, has trouble recognized her family, and constantly mumbles a chant which sounds like "Oh, Maria!" her family describes her as having lost her spirit to remain mentally and physically active, and she is deteriorating rapidly in all respects.

Standard of Care

In September 1986, good and accepted nursing home practice in the field of long-term care required that the authorities of this continued care center do certain things:

1. Have Nurse's Aides be constantly aware that they are handling patients whose bones are brittle and who have difficulty ambulating on their own. Consequently, it is important that the Nurse's Aide not rush the patient in wheelchair and take proper precautions when wheeling the patient in the wheelchair; that she take care not to possibly strike any furniture, or anything which may suddenly appear to be in the way.

2. Controls must be instituted in taking care of patients with limited control of their limbs so that the patient cannot possibly put her foot down to stop the wheelchair when it is being ambulated. The patient's legs should be restrained or even strapped into a wheelchair and covered with some blanket or afghan so that she cannot possibly injure herself if her leg or other parts of the body touch something in the way while in the wheelchair. And it should go without saying that a patient should not have to put her foot down to stop the wheelchair, assuming that is what happened. The aide should slow down or stop at the verbal request of the patient.

The incident report indicated that "to prevent similar incidents, if the incident is due to carelessness, the aide should be asked to be more aware when giving patient care."

Departures from the Standard of Care

The Nursing Staff at this continuing care center in Michigan departed from good and accepted nursing home practice in the following way:

1. They failed to institute controls so that the patient could not possibly put her foot down to stop a wheelchair. It is noted that no remark was made about the patient putting down her foot to stop the wheelchair in either the nurse's notes under the date of September 28, 1986, or in the Incident Report which was drawn up at the time this incident occurred. The Incident Report did indicate that the patient stated that she felt her knee was cracked when she was pushed down the hall in the wheelchair. The hospital record states that the patient was accidentally pushed against the wall, striking her right knee. She had pain in the lateral region of the knee; she had much difficulty in straightening the knee and was in severe pain. Later the hospital found that there was a fracture at the neck of the fibula.

From all indications in the records, this patient was alert and in control of "all" of her mental faculties as mentioned by the physician himself. Though she had previously experienced some heart problems and some bronchial problems with congestion, she was able to function very adequately at the continued care center until the incident on September 28, 1986. After the incident, the records indicate that she was depressed, irritable "her spirit broken," in a difficult mental condition, quieter, had much less to say and was sad. At the nursing home, she never walked again, made no more telephone calls, sent no more cards, was confused insofar that she didn't distinguish between her brother and her nephew, and her mental condition "deteriorated 90% in the first year." It was indicated that the she could not walk due to both mental and physical changes in her condition.

2. While the nursing home acted expeditiously in sending her to the hospital for the examination following the incident on September 28, 1986, apparently she was returned to the continued care center and did not have any surgical care on her fractured knee until several days later. It is indicated in several records that no action was actually taken for seven days and that she was sent back and forth from the continued care center to the hospital. This may have aggravated her deteriorating condition following the cast which was applied to her knee.

3. Under the legal doctrine of Respondeat Superior (See Chapter II), the employer is responsible for the actions of his employees. In this instance, the continued care center must be considered responsible for the actions of its Nurses' Aides, especially B.R., who was taking care of the patient and pushing the wheelchair at the time of her knee fracture. Whether she was going too fast and carelessly hit the wall with the patient, as is indicated by the documents recorded at the time, or whether the patient felt it necessary to put her foot down to stop the wheelchair, as Ms. R. later claims, either scenario represents a breach of the applicable standard of care.

CAUSATIONS

The failure to conform to good and accepted Nursing Home practice was the probable cause of the many changes that have occurred to W.W. since September, 1986. While it is true that a number of years have passed since Ms. W. was injured, it is also true that the changes in her condition occurred immediately after the injury and have progressively gotten worse.

Undoubtedly, the accident in which her knee struck the wall and was fractured caused her physical and mental condition to deteriorate substantially. These charges are noted in the summary of the facts and in the deviation from the standard of care. Deterioration was rapid in all respects, both physical and mental. Previously, she was an alert woman enjoying life. Now she is awaiting death, she is virtually bedridden, spends much of her time sitting in the wheelchair and does not participate in normal activities. She even fails to distinguish between members of her family and does not walk anymore. While it may be said that certain charges would have occurred naturally as she grew older, the injury in September, 1986, substantially accelerated these changes. This case was settled, with the nursing home paying.

This case likewise illustrates the importantance of good nursing care and the need for eliminating any possible slips and falls by patients. Surely many such instances occur in nursing homes, but are rarely brought to trial or settlement.

INDEX

N

O

P

Q

R

S

T

U

W

X